P9-CMF-293

MINCE PIE

CHRISTOPHER MORLEY

MINCE PIE

ADVENTURES ON THE
SUNNY SIDE OF GRUB STREET

BY

CHRISTOPHER MORLEY

ILLUSTRATED BY

WALTER JACK DUNCAN

NEW YORK
GEORGE H. DORAN COMPANY

TO

F. M. AND L. J. M.

INSTRUCTIONS

This book is intended to be read in bed. Please do not attempt to read it anywhere else.

In order to obtain the best results for all concerned do not read a borrowed copy, but buy one. If the bed is a double bed, buy two.

Do not lend a copy under any circumstances, but refer your friends to the nearest bookshop, where they may expiate their curiosity.

Most of these sketches were first printed in the Philadelphia *Evening Public Ledger;* others appeared in *The Bookman,* the Boston *Evening Transcript, Life,* and *The Smart Set.* To all these publications I am indebted for permission to reprint.

If one asks what excuse there can be for prolonging the existence of these trifles, my answer is that there is no excuse. But a copy on

[vii]

Instructions

the bedside shelf may possibly pave the way to easy slumber. Only a mind "debauched by learning" (in Doctor Johnson's phrase) will scrutinize them too anxiously.

It seems to me, on reading the proofs, that the skit entitled "Trials of a President Travelling Abroad" is a faint and subconscious echo of a passage in a favorite of my early youth, *Happy Thoughts*, by the late F. C. Burnand. If this acknowledgment should move anyone to read that delicious classic of pleasantry, the innocent plunder may be pardonable.

And now a word of obeisance. I take this opportunity of thanking several gentle overseers and magistrates who have been too generously friendly to these eccentric gestures. These are Mr. Robert Cortes Holliday, editor of *The Bookman* and victim of the novelette herein entitled "Owd Bob"; Mr. Edwin F. Edgett, literary editor of The Boston *Transcript,* who has often permitted me to cut outrageous capers in his hospitable columns; and Mr. Thomas L. Masson, of *Life,* who allows me to reprint several of the shorter pieces. But most of all I thank Mr. David E. Smiley, editor

[viii]

Instructions

of the Philadelphia *Evening Public Ledger,* for
whom the majority of these sketches were written, and whose patience and kindness have been
a frequent amazement to

THE AUTHOR.

PHILADELPHIA
September, 1919

CONTENTS

Contents

[xii]

Contents

MINCE PIE

MINCE PIE

ON FILLING AN INK-WELL

THOSE who buy their ink in little stone
jugs may prefer to do so because the
pottle reminds them of cruiskeen lawn or gin-
ger beer (with its wire-bound cork), but they
miss a noble delight. Ink should be bought
in the tall, blue glass, quart bottle (with the
ingenious non-drip spout), and once every three
weeks or so, when you fill your ink-well, it is
your privilege to elevate the flask against the
brightness of a window, and meditate (with a
breath of sadness) on the joys and problems
that sacred fluid holds in solution.

How blue it shines toward the light! Blue
as lupin or larkspur, or cornflower—aye, and
even so blue art thou, my scriven, to think
how far the written page falls short of the
bright ecstasy of thy dream! In the bottle,
what magnificence of unpenned stuff lies cool
and liquid: what fluency of essay, what fonts of
song. As the bottle glints, blue as a squill or

a hyacinth, blue as the meadows of Elysium or the eyes of girls loved by young poets, meseems the racing pen might almost gain upon the thoughts that are turning the bend in the road. A jolly throng, those thoughts: I can see them talking and laughing together. But when pen reaches the road's turning, the thoughts are gone far ahead: their delicate figures are silhouettes against the sky.

It is a sacramental matter, this filling the ink-well. Is there a writer, however humble, who has not poured into his writing pot, with the ink, some wistful hopes or prayers for what may emerge from that dark source? Is there not some particular reverence due the ink-well, some form of propitiation to humbug the powers of evil and constraint that devil the journalist? Satan hovers near the ink-pot. Luther solved the matter by throwing the well itself at the apparition. That savors to me too much of homeopathy. If Satan ever puts his face over my desk, I shall hurl a volume of Harold Bell Wright at him.

But what becomes of the ink-pots of glory? The conduit from which Boswell drew, for Charles Dilly in The Poultry, the great river of his Johnson? The well (was it of blue china?) whence flowed *Dream Children: a Revery?* (It was written on folio ledger sheets

[18]

On Filling an Ink-well

from the East India House—I saw the manuscript only yesterday in a room at Daylesford, Pennsylvania, where much of the richest ink of the last two centuries is lovingly laid away.) The pot of chuckling fluid where Harry Fielding dipped his pen to tell the history of a certain foundling; the ink-wells of the Café de la

Source on the Boul' Mich'—do they by any chance remember which it was that R. L. S. used? One of the happiest tremors of my life was when I went to that café and called for a bock and writing material, just because R. L. S. had once written letters there. And the ink-well Poe used at that boarding-house in Greenwich Street, New York (April, 1844), when he wrote to his dear Muddy (his mother-in-law) to describe how he and Virginia had reached a haven of square meals. That hopeful letter, so perfect now in pathos—

For breakfast we had excellent-flavored coffee, hot and strong—not very clear and no great deal of

[19]

cream—veal cutlets, elegant ham and eggs and nice bread and butter. I never sat down to a more plentiful or a nicer breakfast. I wish you could have seen the eggs—and the great dishes of meat. Sis [his wife] is delighted, and we are both in excellent spirits. She has coughed hardly any and had no night sweat. She is now busy mending my pants, which I tore against a nail. I went out last night and bought a skein of silk, a skein of thread, two buttons, a pair of slippers, and a tin pan for the stove. The fire kept in all night. We have now got four dollars and a half left. To-morrow I am going to try and borrow three dollars, so that I may have a fortnight to go upon. I feel in excellent spirits, and haven't drank a drop—so that I hope soon to get out of trouble.

Yes, let us clear the typewriter off the table: an ink-well is a sacred thing.

Do you ever stop to think, when you see the grimy spattered desks of a public post-office, how many eager or puzzled human hearts have tried, in those dingy little ink-cups, to set themselves right with fortune? What blissful meetings have been appointed, what scribblings of pain and sorrow, out of those founts of common speech. And the ink-wells on hotel counters—does not the public dipping place of the Bellevue Hotel, Boston, win a new dignity in my memory when I know (as I learned lately) that Rupert Brooke registered there in the

On Filling an Ink-well

spring of 1914? I remember, too, a certain pleasant vibration when, signing my name one day in the Bellevue's book, I found Miss Agnes Repplier's autograph a little above on the same page.

Among our younger friends, Vachel Lindsay comes to mind as one who has done honor to the ink-well. His *Apology for the Bottle Volcanic* is in his best flow of secret smiling (save an unfortunate dilution of Riley):

Sometimes I dip my pen and find the bottle full of
    fire,
The salamanders flying forth I cannot but ad-
    mire. . . .
O sad deceiving ink, as bad as liquor in its way—
All demons of a bottle size have pranced from you
    to-day,
And seized my pen for hobby-horse as witches ride
    a broom,
And left a trail of brimstone words and blots and
    gobs of gloom.
And yet when I am extra good . . . [*here I omit
    the transfusion of Riley*]
My bottle spreads a rainbow mist, and from the
    vapor fine
Ten thousand troops from fairyland come riding in
    a line.

I suppose it is the mark of a trifling mind, yet I like to hear of the little particulars that surrounded those whose pens struck sparks.

[21]

Mince Pie

It is Boswell that leads us into that habit of thought. I like to know what the author wore, how he sat, what the furniture of his desk and chamber, who cooked his meals for him, and with what appetite he approached them. "The mind soars by an effort to the grand and lofty" (so dipped Hazlitt in some favored ink-bottle) —"it is at home in the groveling, the disagreeable, and the little."

I like to think, as I look along book shelves, that every one of these favorites was born out of an ink-well. I imagine the hopes and visions that thronged the author's mind as he filled his pot and sliced the quill. What various fruits have flowed from those ink-wells of the past: for some, comfort and honor, quiet homes and plenteousness; for others, bitterness and disappointment. I have seen a copy of Poe's poems, published in 1845 by Putnam, inscribed by the author. The volume had been bought for $2,500. Think what that would have meant to Poe himself.

Some such thoughts as these twinkled in my head as I held up the Pierian bottle against the light, admired the deep blue of it, and filled my ink-well. And then I took up my pen, which wrote:

A GRACE BEFORE WRITING

On Filling an Ink-well

This is a sacrament, I think!
  Holding the bottle toward the light,
As blue as lupin gleams the ink:
  May Truth be with me as I write!

That small dark cistern may afford
  Reunion with some vanished friend,—
And with this ink I have just poured
  May none but honest words be penned!

OLD THOUGHTS FOR CHRISTMAS

A NEW thought for Christmas? Who ever wanted a new thought for Christmas? That man should be shot who would try to brain one. It is an impertinence even to write about Christmas. Christmas is a matter that humanity has taken so deeply to heart that we will not have our festival meddled with by bungling hands. No efficiency expert would dare tell us that Christmas is inefficient; that the clockwork toys will soon be broken; that no one can eat a peppermint cane a yard long; that the curves on our chart of kindness should be ironed out so that the "peak load" of December would be evenly distributed through the year. No sour-

[24]

Old Thoughts for Christmas

face dare tell us that we drive postmen and shopgirls into Bolshevism by overtaxing them with our frenzied purchasing or that it is absurd to send to a friend in a steam-heated apartment in a prohibition republic a bright little picture card of a gentleman in Georgian costume drinking ale by a roaring fire of logs. None in his senses, I say, would emit such sophistries, for Christmas is a law unto itself and is not conducted by card-index. Even the postmen and shopgirls, severe though their labors, would not have matters altered. There is none of us who does not enjoy hardship and bustle that contribute to the happiness of others.

There is an efficiency of the heart that transcends and contradicts that of the head. Things of the spirit differ from things material in that the more you give the more you have. The comedian has an immensely better time than the audience. To modernize the adage, to give is more fun than to receive. Especially if you have wit enough to give to those who don't expect it. Surprise is the most primitive joy of humanity. Surprise is the first reason for a baby's laughter. And at Christmas time, when we are all a little childish I hope, surprise is the flavor of our keenest joys. We all remember the thrill with which we once heard, behind some closed door, the rustle and

[25]

crackle of paper parcels being tied up. We knew that we were going to be surprised—a delicious refinement and luxuriant seasoning of the emotion!

Christmas, then, conforms to this deeper efficiency of the heart. We are not methodical in kindness; we do not "fill orders" for consignments of affection. We let our kindness ramble and explore; old forgotten friendships pop up in our minds and we mail a card to Harry Hunt, of Minneapolis (from whom we have not heard for half a dozen years), "just to surprise him." A business man who shipped a carload of goods to a customer, just to surprise him, would soon perish of abuse. But no one ever refuses a shipment of kindness, because no one ever feels overstocked with it. It is coin of the realm, current everywhere. And we do not try to measure our kindnesses to the capacity of our friends. Friendship is not measurable in calories. How many times this year have you "turned" your stock of kindness?

It is the gradual approach to the Great Surprise that lends full savor to the experience. It has been thought by some that Christmas would gain in excitement if no one knew when it was to be; if (keeping the festival within the winter months) some public functionary (say, Mr. Burleson) were to announce some unexpected morning, "A week from to-day will be Christmas!" Then what a scurrying and joyful frenzy—what a festooning of shops and mad purchasing of presents! But it would not be half the fun of the slow approach of the familiar date. All through November and December we watch it drawing nearer; we see the shop windows begin to glow with red and green and lively colors; we note the altered demeanor of bellboys and janitors as the Date flows quietly toward us; we pass through the haggard perplexity of "Only Four Days More" when we suddenly realize it is too late to make our shopping the display of lucid affectionate reasoning we had contemplated, and clutch wildly at grotesque tokens—and then (sweetest of all) comes the quiet calmness of Christmas Eve. Then, while we decorate the tree or carry parcels of tissue paper and red ribbon to a carefully prepared list of aunts and godmothers, or reckon up a little pile of bright quarters on the dining-room table in preparation for to-morrow's largesse—then it is that the brief, poignant and precious sweetness of the experience claims us at the full. Then we can see that all our careful wisdom and shrewdness were folly and stupidity; and we can understand the meaning of that Great Surprise—that where we planned wealth we found ourselves poor; that where we

[27]

thought to be impoverished we were enriched.
The world is built upon a lovely plan if we take
time to study the blue-prints of the heart.

Humanity must be forgiven much for having
invented Christmas. What does it matter that
a great poet and philosopher urges "the aban-
donment of the masculine pronoun in allusions
to the First or Fundamental Energy"? The-
ology is not saddled upon pronouns; the best
doctrine is but three words, God is Love. Love,
or kindness, is fundamental energy enough to
satisfy any brooder. And Christmas Day means
the birth of a child; that is to say, the triumph
of life and hope over suffering.

Just for a few hours on Christmas Eve and
Christmas Day the stupid, harsh mechanism
of the world runs down and we permit ourselves to live according to untrammeled common sense, the unconquerable efficiency of good
will. We grant ourselves the complete and
selfish pleasure of loving others better than ourselves. How odd it seems, how unnaturally
happy we are! We feel there must be some
mistake, and rather yearn for the familiar fric-
tions and distresses. Just for a few hours we
"purge out of every heart the lurking grudge."
We know then that hatred is a form of illness;
that suspicion and pride are only fear; that the
rascally acts of others are perhaps, in the queer

Old Thoughts for Christmas

webwork of human relations, due to some cal-
ousness of our own. Who knows? Some man
may have robbed a bank in Nashville or fired
a gun in Louvain because we looked so intol-
erably smug in Philadelphia!

So at Christmas we tap that vast reservoir
of wisdom and strength—call it efficiency or the
fundamental energy if you will—Kindness.
And our kindness, thank heaven, is not the
placid kindness of angels; it is veined with
human blood; it is full of absurdities, irrita-
tions, frustrations. A man 100 per cent. kind
would be intolerable. As a wise teacher said,
the milk of human kindness easily curdles into
cheese. We like our friends' affections because
we know the tincture of mortal acid is in them.
We remember the satirist who remarked that to
love one's self is the beginning of a lifelong
romance. We know this lifelong romance will
resume its sway; we shall lose our tempers, be
obstinate, peevish and crank. We shall fidget
and fume while waiting our turn in the barber's
chair; we shall argue and muddle and mope.
And yet, for a few hours, what a happy vision
that was! And we turn, on Christmas Eve, to
pages which those who speak our tongue immor-
tally associate with the season—the pages of
Charles Dickens. Love of humanity endures as
long as the thing it loves, and those pages are

packed as full of it as a pound cake is full of fruit. A pound cake will keep moist three years; a sponge cake is dry in three days.

And now humanity has its most beautiful and most appropriate Christmas gift—Peace. The Magi of Versailles and Washington having unwound for us the tissue paper and red ribbon (or red tape) from this greatest of all gifts, let us in days to come measure up to what has been born through such anguish and horror. If war is illness and peace is health, let us remember also that health is not merely a blessing to be received intact once and for all. It is not a substance but a condition, to be maintained only by sound régime, self-discipline and simplicity. Let the Wise Men not be too wise; let them remember those other Wise Men who, after their long journey and their sage surmisings, found only a Child. On this evening it serves us nothing to pile up filing cases and rolltop desks toward the stars, for in our city square the Star itself has fallen, and shines upon the Tree.

CHRISTMAS CARDS

BY a stroke of good luck we found a little
shop where a large overstock of Christmas
cards was selling at two for five. The original
5's and 10's were still penciled on them, and
while we were debating whether to rub them
off a thought occurred to us. When will artists and printers design us some Christmas
cards that will be honest and appropriate to
the time we live in? Never was the Day of
Peace and Good Will so full of meaning as this
year; and never did the little cards, charming
as they were, seem so formal, so merely pretty,
so devoid of imagination, so inadequate to the
festival.

This is an age of strange and stirring beauty,
of extraordinary romance and adventure, of new
joys and pains. And yet our Christmas artists
have nothing more to offer us than the old
formalism of Yuletide convention. After a
considerable amount of searching in the bazaars
we have found not one Christmas card that
showed even a glimmering of the true romance,
which is to see the beauty or wonder or peril

that lies around us. Most of the cards hark back to the stage-coach up to its hubs in snow, or the blue bird, with which Maeterlinck penalized us (what has a blue bird got to do with Christmas?), or the open fireplace and jug of mulled claret. Now these things are merry enough in their way, or they were once upon a time; but we plead for an honest romanticism in Christmas cards that will express something of the entrancing color and circumstance that surround us to-day. Is not a commuter's train, stalled in a drift, far more lively to our hearts than the mythical stage-coach? Or an interurban trolley winging its way through the dusk like a casket of golden light? Or even a country flivver, loaded down with parcels and holly and the Yuletide keg of root beer? Root beer may be but meager flaggonage compared to mulled claret, but at any rate 'tis honest, 'tis actual, 'tis tangible and potable. And where, among all the Christmas cards, is the airplane, that most marvelous and heart-seizing of all our triumphs? Where is the stately apartment house, looming like Gibraltar against a sunset sky? Must we, even at Christmas time, fool ourselves with a picturesqueness that is gone, seeing nothing of what is around us?

It is said that man's material achievements have outrun his imagination; that poets and

[32]

painters are too puny to grapple with the world as it is. Certainly a visitor from another sphere, looking on our fantastic and exciting civilization, would find little reflection of it in the Christmas card. He would find us clinging desperately to what we have been taught to believe was picturesque and jolly, and afraid to assert that the things of to-day are comely too. Even on the basis of discomfort (an acknowledged criterion of picturesqueness) surely a trolley car jammed with parcel-laden passengers is just as satisfying a spectacle as any stage coach? Surely the steam radiator, if not so lovely as a flame-gilded hearth, is more real to most of us? And instead of the customary picture of shivering subjects of George III held up by a highwayman on Hampstead Heath, why not a deftly delineated sketch of victims in a steam-heated lobby submitting to the plunder of the hat-check bandit? Come, let us be honest! The romance of to-day is as good as any!

Many must have felt this same uneasiness in trying to find Christmas cards that would really say something of what is in their hearts. The sentiment behind the card is as lovely and as true as ever, but the cards themselves are outmoded bottles for the new wine. It seems a cruel thing to say, but we are impatient with the mottoes and pictures we see in the shops

[33]

because they are a conventional echo of a beauty that is past. What could be more absurd than to send to a friend in a city apartment a rhyme such as this:

> As round the Christmas fire you sit
> And hear the bells with frosty chime,
> Think, friendship that long love has knit
> Grows sweeter still at Christmas time!

If that is sent to the janitor or the elevator boy we have no cavil, for these gentlemen do actually see a fire and hear bells ring; but the apartment tenant hears naught but the hissing of the steam in the radiator, and counts himself lucky to hear that. Why not be honest and say to him:

> I hope the janitor has shipped
> You steam, to keep the cold away;
> And if the hallboys have been tipped,
> Then joy be thine on Christmas Day!

We had not meant to introduce this jocular note into our meditation, for we are honestly aggrieved that so many of the Christmas cards hark back to an old tradition that is gone, and never attempt to express any of the romance of to-day. You may protest that Christmas is the oldest thing in the world, which is true; yet it is also new every year, and never newer than now.

[34]

ON UNANSWERING LETTERS

THERE are a great many people who really believe in answering letters the day they are received, just as there are people who go to the movies at 9 o'clock in the morning; but these people are stunted and queer.

It is a great mistake. Such crass and breathless promptness takes away a great deal of the pleasure of correspondence.

The psychological didoes involved in receiving letters and making up one's mind to answer them are very complex. If the tangled process could be clearly analyzed and its component involutions isolated for inspection we might reach a clearer comprehension of that curious bag of tricks, the efficient Masculine Mind.

Take Bill F., for instance, a man so delight-

Mince Pie

ful that even to contemplate his existence puts us in good humor and makes us think well of a world that can exhibit an individual equally comely in mind, body and estate. Every now and then we get a letter from Bill, and immediately we pass into a kind of trance, in which our mind rapidly enunciates the ideas, thoughts, surmises and contradictions that we would like to write to him in reply. We think what fun it would be to sit right down and churn the ink-well, spreading speculation and cynicism over a number of sheets of foolscap to be wafted Billward.

Sternly we repress the impulse for we know that the shock to Bill of getting so immediate a retort would surely unhinge the well-fitted panels of his intellect.

We add his letter to the large delta of unanswered mail on our desk, taking occasion to turn the mass over once or twice and run through it in a brisk, smiling mood, thinking of all the jolly letters we shall write some day.

After Bill's letter has lain on the pile for a fortnight or so it has been gently silted over by about twenty other pleasantly postponed manuscripts. Coming upon it by chance, we reflect that any specific problems raised by Bill in that manifesto will by this time have settled themselves. And his random speculations upon household management and human destiny will probably have taken a new slant by now, so that to answer his letter in its own tune will not be congruent with his present fevers. We had better bide a wee until we really have something of circumstance to impart.

We wait a week.

By this time a certain sense of shame has begun to invade the privacy of our brain. We feel that to answer that letter now would be an indelicacy. Better to pretend that we never got it. By and by Bill will write again and then we will answer promptly. We put the letter back in the middle of the heap and think what a fine chap Bill is. But he knows we love him, so it doesn't really matter whether we write or not.

Another week passes by, and no further communication from Bill. We wonder whether he does love us as much as we thought. Still— we are too proud to write and ask.

A few days later a new thought strikes us. Perhaps Bill thinks we have died and he is annoyed because he wasn't invited to the funeral. Ought we to wire him? No, because after all we are not dead, and even if he thinks we are, his subsequent relief at hearing the good news of our survival will outweigh his bitterness during the interval. One of these days we will write him a letter that will really express our heart, filled with all the grindings and gear-work of our mind, rich in affection and fallacy. But we had better let it ripen and mellow for a while. Letters, like wines, accumulate bright fumes and bubblings if kept under cork.

Presently we turn over that pile of letters again. We find in the lees of the heap two or three that have gone for six months and can safely be destroyed. Bill is still on our mind, but in a pleasant, dreamy kind of way. He does not ache or twinge us as he did a month ago. It is fine to have old friends like that and keep in touch with them. We wonder how he is and whether he has two children or three. Splendid old Bill!

By this time we have written Bill several letters in imagination and enjoyed doing so, but the matter of sending him an actual letter has begun to pall. The thought no longer has the savor and vivid sparkle it had once. When one feels like that it is unwise to write. Letters should be spontaneous outpourings: they should never be undertaken merely from a sense of duty. We know that Bill wouldn't want to get a letter that was dictated by a feeling of obligation.

Another fortnight or so elapsing, it occurs to

On Unanswering Letters

us that we have entirely forgotten what Bill
said to us in that letter. We take it out and
con it over. Delightful fellow! It is full of
his own felicitous kinks of whim, though some
of it sounds a little old-fashioned by now.
It seems a bit stale, has lost some of its fresh-
ness and surprise. Better not answer it just
yet, for Christmas will soon be here and we
shall have to write then anyway. We wonder,
can Bill hold out until Christmas without a
letter?

We have been rereading some of those im-
aginary letters to Bill that have been dancing
in our head. They are full of all sorts of fine
stuff. If Bill ever gets them he will know
how we love him. To use O. Henry's immortal
joke, we have days of Damon and Knights of
Pythias writing those uninked letters to Bill.
A curious thought has come to us. Perhaps it
would be better if we never saw Bill again.
It is very difficult to talk to a man when you
like him so much. It is much easier to write
in the sweet fantastic strain. We are so in-
articulate when face to face. If Bill comes to
town we will leave word that we have gone
away. Good old Bill! He will always be a
precious memory.

A few days later a sudden frenzy sweeps
over us, and though we have many pressing

[39]

matters on hand, we mobilize pen and paper and literary shock troops and prepare to hurl several battalions at Bill. But, strangely enough our utterance seems stilted and stiff. We have nothing to say. *My dear Bill,* we begin, *seems a long time since we heard from you. Why don't you write? We still love you, in spite of all your shortcomings.*

That doesn't seem very cordial. We mull over the pen and nothing comes. Bursting with affection, we are unable to say a word.

Just then the phone rings. "Hello?" we say.

It is Bill, come to town unexpectedly.

"Good old fish!" we cry, ecstatic. "Meet you at the corner of Tenth and Chestnut in five minutes."

We tear up the unfinished letter. Bill will never know how much we love him. Perhaps it is just as well. It is very embarrassing to have your friends know how you feel about them. When we meet him we will be a little bit on our guard. It would not be well to be betrayed into any extravagance of cordiality.

And perhaps a not altogether false little story could be written about a man who never visited those most dear to him, because it panged him so to say good-bye when he had to leave.

A LETTER TO FATHER TIME

(NEW YEAR'S EVE)

DEAR Father Time—This is your night of triumph, and it seems only fair to pay you a little tribute. Some people, in a noble mood of bravado, consider New Year's Eve an occasion of festivity. Long, long in advance they reserve a table at their favorite café; and becomingly habited in boiled shirts or gowns of the lowest visibility, and well armed with a commodity which is said to be synonymous with yourself—money—they seek to outwit you by crowding a month of merriment into half a dozen hours. Yet their victory is brief and fallacious, for if hours spin too fast by night they will move grindingly on the axle the next morning. None of us can beat you in the end. Even the hat-check boy grows old, becomes gray and dies at last babbling of greenbacks.

To my own taste, old Time, it is more agreeable to make this evening a season of gruesome brooding. Morosely I survey the faults and

[41]

Mince Pie

follies of my last year. I am grown too canny to pour the new wine of good resolution into the old bottles of my imperfect humors. But I get a certain grim satisfaction in thinking how we all—every human being of us—share alike in bondage to your oppression. There is the only true and complete democracy, the only absolute brotherhood of man. The great ones of the earth—Charley Chaplin and Douglas Fairbanks, General Pershing and Miss Amy Lowell—all these are in service to the same tyranny. Day after day slips or jolts past, joins the Great Majority; suddenly we wake with a start to find that the best of it is gone by. Surely it seems but a day ago that Stevenson set out to write a little book that was to be called "Life at Twenty-five"—before he got it written he was long past the delectable age— and now we rub our eyes and see he has been dead longer than the span of life he then so delightfully contemplated. If there is one meditation common to every adult on this globe it is this, so variously phrased, "Well, bo, Time sure does hustle."

Some of them have scurvily entreated you, old Time! The thief of youth, they have called you; a highwayman, a gipsy, a grim reaper. It seems a little unfair. For you have your kindly moods, too. Without your gentle pas-

A Letter to Father Time

sage where were Memory, the sweetest of
lesser pleasures? You are the only medicine for
many a woe, many a sore heart. And surely you
have a right to reap where you alone have sown?
Our strength, our wit, our comeliness, all those
virtues and graces that you pilfer with such
gentle hand, did you not give them to us in the
first place? Give, do I say? Nay, we knew,
even as we clutched them, they were but a loan.
And the great immortality of the race endures,
for every day that we see taken away from ourselves we see added to our children or our
grandchildren. It was Shakespeare, who
thought a great deal about you, who put it
best:

Nativity, once in the main of light,
  Crawls to maturity, wherewith being crowned,
Crooked eclipses 'gainst his glory fight
  And Time that gave doth now his gift confound—

It is to be hoped, my dear Time, that you
have read Shakespeare's sonnets, because they
will teach you a deal about the dignity of your
career, and also suggest to you the only way
we have of keeping up with you. There is no
way of outwitting Time, Shakespeare tells his
young friend, "Save breed to brave him when
he takes thee hence." Or, as a poor bungling
parodist revamped it:

[43]

Mince Pie

Pep is the stuff to put Old Time on skids—
Pep in your copy, yes, and lots of kids.

It is true that Shakespeare hints another way of doing you in, which is to write sonnets as good as his. This way, needless to add, is open to few.

Well, my dear Time, you are not going to fool me into making myself ridiculous this New Year's Eve with a lot of bonny but impossible resolutions. I know that you are playing with me just as a cat plays with a mouse; yet even the most piteous mousekin sometimes causes his tormentor surprise or disappointment by getting under a bureau or behind the stove, where, for the moment, she cannot paw him. Every now and then, with a little luck, I shall pull off just such a scurry into temporary immortality. It may come by reading Dickens or by seeing a sunset, or by lunching with friends, or by forgetting to wind the alarm clock, or by contemplating the rosy little pate of my daughter, who is still only a nine days' wonder—so young that she doesn't even know what you are doing to her. But you are not going to have the laugh on me by luring me into resolutions. I know my weaknesses. I know that I shall probably continue to annoy newsdealers by reading the magazines on the

[44]

A Letter to Father Time

stalls instead of buying them; that I shall put off having my hair cut; drop tobacco cinders on my waistcoat; feel bored at the idea of having to shave and get dressed; be nervous when the gas burner pops when turned off; buy more Liberty Bonds than I can afford and have to hock them at a grievous loss. I shall continue to be pleasant to insurance agents, from sheer

lack of manhood; and to keep library books out over the date and so incur a fine. My only hope, you see, is resolutely to determine to persist in these failings. Then, by sheer perversity, I may grow out of them.

What avail, indeed, for any of us to make good resolutions when one contemplates the grand pageant of human frailty? Observe what I noticed the other day in the Lost and Found column of the New York *Times:*

[45]

Mince Pie

Surely, if Mr. Flint could not remember to keep his teeth in his mouth, or if any one else was so basely whimsical as to juggle them away from him, it may well teach us to be chary of extravagant hopes for the future. Even the League of Nations, when one contemplates the sad case of Mr. Flint, becomes a rather anemic safeguard. We had better keep Mr. Flint in mind through the New Year as a symbol of human error and disappointment. And the best of it is, my dear Time, that you, too, may be a little careless. Perhaps one of these days you may doze a little and we shall steal a few hours of timeless bliss. Shall we see a little ad in the papers:

Well, my dear Time, we approach the Zero Hour. I hope you will have a Happy New Year, and conduct yourself with becoming restraint. So live, my dear fellow, that we may say, "A good Time was enjoyed by all." As

A Letter to Father Time

the hands of the clock go over the top and into the No Man's Land of the New Year, good luck to you!

Your obedient servant!

WHAT MEN LIVE BY

WHAT a delicate and rare and gracious art is the art of conversation! With what a dexterity and skill the bubble of speech must be maneuvered if mind is to meet and mingle with mind.

There is no sadder disappointment than to realize that a conversation has been a complete failure. By which we mean that it has failed in blending or isolating for contrast the ideas, opinions and surmises of two eager minds. So often a conversation is shipwrecked by the very eagerness of one member to contribute. There must be give and take, parry and thrust, patience to hear and judgment to utter. How uneasy is the qualm as one looks back on an hour's talk and sees that the opportunity was wasted; the precious instant of intercourse gone forever: the secrets of the heart still incommunicate! Perhaps we were too anxious to hurry the moment, to enforce our own theory, to adduce instance from our own experience. Perhaps we were not patient enough to wait

[48]

until our friend could express himself with ease and happiness. Perhaps we squandered the dialogue in tangent topics, in a multitude of irrelevances.

How few, how few are those gifted for real talk! There are fine merry fellows, full of mirth and shrewdly minted observation, who will not abide by one topic, who must always be lashing out upon some new byroad, snatching at every bush they pass. They are too excit-

able, too ungoverned for the joys of patient intercourse. Talk is so solemn a rite it should be approached with prayer and must be conducted with nicety and forbearance. What steadiness and sympathy are needed if the thread of thought is to be unwound without tangles or snapping! What forbearance, while each of the pair, after tentative gropings here and yonder, feels his way toward truth as he sees it. So often two in talk are like men standing back to back, each trying to describe to the other what he sees and disputing because

[49]

their visions do not tally. It takes a little time for minds to turn face to face.

Very often conversations are better among three than between two, for the reason that then one of the trio is always, unconsciously, acting as umpire, interposing fair play, recalling wandering wits to the nub of the argument, seeing that the aggressiveness of one does no foul to the reticence of another. Talk in twos may, alas! fall into speaker and listener: talk in threes rarely does so.

It is little realized how slowly, how painfully, we approach the expression of truth. We are so variable, so anxious to be polite, and alternately swayed by caution or anger. Our mind oscillates like a pendulum: it takes some time for it to come to rest. And then, the proper allowance and correction has to be made for our individual vibrations that prevent accuracy. Even the compass needle doesn't point the true north, but only the magnetic north. Similarly our minds at best can but indicate magnetic truth, and are distorted by many things that act as iron filings do on the compass. The necessity of holding one's job: what an iron filing that is on the compass card of a man's brain!

We are all afraid of truth: we keep a battalion of our pet prejudices and precautions ready to throw into the argument as shock troops, rather than let our fortress of Truth be stormed. We have smoke bombs and decoy ships and all manner of cunning colorizations by which we conceal our innards from our friends, and even from ourselves. How we fume and fidget, how we bustle and dodge rather than commit ourselves.

In days of hurry and complication, in the incessant pressure of human problems that thrust our days behind us, does one never dream of a way of life in which talk would be honored and exalted to its proper place in the sun? What a zest there is in that intimate unreserved exchange of thought, in the pursuit of the magical blue bird of joy and human satisfaction that may be seen flitting distantly through the branches of life. It was a sad thing for the world when it grew so busy that men had no time to talk. There are such treasures of knowledge and compassion in the minds of our friends, could we only have time to talk them out of their shy quarries. If we had our way, we would set aside one day a week for talking. In fact, we would reorganize the week altogether. We would have one day for Worship (let each man devote it to worship of whatever he holds dearest); one day for Work; one day for Play (probably fishing);

[51]

one day for Talking; one day for Reading, and one day for Smoking and Thinking. That would leave one day for Resting, and (incidentally) interviewing employers.

The best week of our life was one in which we did nothing but talk. We spent it with a delightful gentleman who has a little bungalow on the shore of a lake in Pike County. He had a great many books and cigars, both of which are conversational stimulants. We used to lie out on the edge of the lake, in our oldest trousers, and talk. We discussed ever so many subjects; in all of them he knew immensely more than we did. We built up a complete philosophy of indolence and good will, according to Food and Sleep and Swimming their proper share of homage. We rose at 10 in the morning and began talking; we talked all day and until 3 o'clock at night. Then we went to bed and regained strength and combativeness for the coming day. Never was a week better spent. We committed no crimes, planned no secret treaties, devised no annexations or indemnities. We envied no one. We examined the entire world and found it worth while. Meanwhile our wives, who were watching (perhaps with a little quiet indignation) from the veranda, kept on asking us, "What on earth do you talk about?"

[52]

What Men Live By

Bless their hearts, men don't have to have anything to talk *about*. They just talk.

And there is only one rule for being a good talker: learn how to listen.

THE UNNATURAL NATURALIST

IT gives us a great deal of pleasure to announce, officially, that spring has arrived.

Our statement is not based on any irrelevant data as to equinoxes or bluebirds or bock-beer signs, but is derived from the deepest authority we know anything about, our subconscious self. We remember that some philosopher, perhaps it was Professor James, suggested that individuals are simply peaks of self-consciousness rising out of the vast ocean of collective human Mind in which we all swim, and are, at bottom, one. Whenever we have to decide any important matter, such as when to get our hair cut and whether to pay a bill or not, and whether to call for the check or let the other fellow do so, we don't attempt to harass our conscious volition with these decisions. We rely on our subconscious and instinctive person, and for better or worse we have to trust to its righteousness and good sense. We just find ourself doing something and we carry on and hope it is for the best.

From this deep abyss of subconsciousness we

The Unnatural Naturalist

learn that it is spring. The mottled goosebone
of the Allentown prophet is no more meteoro-
logically accurate than our subconscience. And
this is how it works.

Once a year, about the approach of the vernal equinox or the seedsman's catalogue, we
wake up at 6 o'clock in the morning. This is
an immediate warning and apprisement that
something is adrift. Three hundred and sixty-
four days in the year we wake, placidly enough,
at seven-ten, ten minutes after the alarm clock
has jangled. But on this particular day,
whether it be the end of February or the middle of March, we wake with the old recogniz-
able nostalgia. It is the last polyp or vestige
of our anthropomorphic and primal self, trail-
ing its pathetic little wisp of glory for the one
day of the whole calendar. All the rest of the
year we are the plodding percheron of com-
merce, patiently tugging our wain; but on that
morning there wambles back, for the nonce,
the pang of Eden. We wake at 6 o'clock; it
is a blue and golden morning and we feel it
imperative to get outdoors as quickly as possible. Not for an instant do we feel the customary respectable and sanctioned desire to kiss
the sheets yet an hour or so. The traipsing,
trolloping humor of spring is in our veins; we
feel that we must be about felling an aurochs

[55]

or a narwhal for breakfast. We leap into our
clothes and hurry downstairs and out of the
front door and skirmish round the house to see
and smell and feel.

It is spring. It is unmistakably spring, because the pewit bushes are budding and on
yonder aspen we can hear a forsythia bursting
into song. It is spring, when the feet of the
floorwalker pain him and smoking-car windows
have to be pried open with chisels. We skip
lightheartedly round the house to see if those
bobolink bulbs we planted are showing any signs
yet, and discover the whisk brush that fell out
of the window last November. And then the
newsboy comes along the street and sees us
prancing about and we feel sheepish and
ashamed and hurry indoors again.

There may still be blizzards and frozen
plumbings and tumbles on icy pavements, but
when that morning of annunciation has come
to us we know that winter is truly dead, even
though his ghost may walk and gibber once or
twice. The sweet urge of the new season has
rippled up through the oceanic depths of our
subconsciousness, and we are aware of the rising tide. Like Mr. Wordsworth we feel that
we are wiser than we know. (Perhaps we have
misquoted that, but let it stand.)

There are other troubles that spring brings

us. We are pitifully ashamed of our ignorance
of nature, and though we try to hide it we keep
getting tripped up. About this time of year
inquisitive persons are always asking us: "Have
you heard any song sparrows yet?" or "Are
there any robins out your way?" or "When do
the laburnums begin to nest out in Marathon?"
Now we really can't tell these people our true

feeling, which is that we do not believe in peek-
ing in on the privacy of the laburnums or any
other songsters. It seems to us really immodest
to keep on spying on the birds in that way. And
as for the bushes and trees, what we want to
know is, How does one ever get to know them?
How do you find out which is an alder and
what is an elm? Or a narcissus and a hyacinth,
does any one really know them apart? We
think it's all a bluff. And jonquils. There was
a nest of them on our porch, we are told, but

we didn't think it any business of ours to bother them. Let nature alone and she'll let you alone.

But there is a pettifogging cult about that says you ought to know these things; moreover, children keep on asking one. We always answer at random and say it's a wagtail or a flowering shrike or a female magnolia. We were brought up in the country and learned that first principle of good manners, which is to let birds and flowers and animals go on about their own affairs without pestering them by asking them their names and addresses. Surely that's what Shakespeare meant by saying a rose by any other name will smell as sweet. We can enjoy a rose just as much as any one, even if we may think it's a hydrangea.

And then we are much too busy to worry about robins and bluebirds and other poultry of that sort. Of course, if we see one hanging about the lawn and it looks hungry we have decency enough to throw out a bone or something for it, but after all we have a lot of troubles of our own to bother about. We are short-sighted, too, and if we try to get near enough to see if it is a robin or only a bandanna some one has dropped, why either it flies away before we get there or it does turn out to be a bandanna or a clothespin. One of

The Unnatural Naturalist

our friends kept on talking about a Baltimore oriole she had seen near our house, and described it as a beautiful yellowish fowl. We felt quite ashamed to be so ignorant, and when one day we thought we saw one near the front porch we left what we were doing, which was writing a check for the coal man, and went out to stalk it. After much maneuvering we got near, made a dash—and it was a banana peel! The oriole had gone back to Baltimore the day before.

We love to read about the birds and flowers and shrubs and insects in poetry, and it makes us very happy to know they are all round us, innocent little things like mice and centipedes and goldenrods (until hay fever time), but as for prying into their affairs we simply won't do it.

SITTING IN THE BARBER'S CHAIR

ONCE every ten weeks or so we get our hair cut.

We are not generally parsimonious of our employer's time, but somehow we do hate to squander that thirty-three minutes, which is the exact chronicide involved in despoiling our skull of a ten weeks' garner. If we were to have our hair cut at the end of eight weeks the shearing would take only thirty-one minutes; but we can never bring ourselves to rob our employer of that much time until we reckon he is really losing prestige by our unkempt appearance. Of course, we believe in having our hair cut during office hours. That is the only device we know to make the hateful operation tolerable.

To the times mentioned above should be added fifteen seconds, which is the slice of eternity needed to trim, prune and chasten our mustache, which is not a large group of foliage.

We knew a traveling man who never got his hair cut except when he was on the road, which permitted him to include the transaction in his

[60]

Sitting in the Barber's Chair

expense account; but somehow it seems to us more ethical to steal time than to steal money.

We like to view this whole matter in a philosophical and ultra-pragmatic way. Some observers have hazarded that our postponement of haircuts is due to mere lethargy and inertia, but that is not so. Every time we get our locks shorn our wife tells us that we have got them too short. She says that our head has a very homely and bourgeois bullet shape, a sort of pithecanthropoid contour, which is revealed by a close trim. After five weeks' growth, however, we begin to look quite distinguished. The difficulty then is to ascertain just when the law of diminishing returns comes into play. When do we cease to look distinguished and begin to appear merely slovenly? Careful study has taught us that this begins to take place at the end of sixty-five days, in warm weather. Add five days or so for natural procrastination and devilment, and we have seventy days interval, which we have posited as the ideal orbit for our tonsorial ecstasies.

When at last we have hounded ourself into robbing our employer of those thirty-three minutes, plus fifteen seconds for you know what, we find ourself in the barber's chair. Despairingly we gaze about at the little blue flasks with flowers enameled on them; at the piles of clean

Mince Pie

towels; at the bottles of mandrake essence which we shall presently have to affirm or deny. Under any other circumstances we should deeply enjoy a half hour spent in a comfortable chair, with nothing to do but do nothing. Our barber is a delightful fellow; he looks benign and does not prattle; he respects the lobes of our ears and other vulnerabilia. But for some inscrutable reason we feel strangely ill at ease in his chair. We can't think of anything to think about. Blankly we brood in the hope of catching the hem of some intimation of immortality. But no, there is nothing to do but sit there, useless as an incubator with no eggs in it. The processes of wasting and decay are hurrying us rapidly to a pauperish grave, every instant brings us closer to a notice in the obit column, and yet we sit and sit without two worthy thoughts to rub against each other.

Oh, the poverty of mortal mind, the sad meagerness of the human soul! Here we are, a vital, breathing entity, transformed to a mere chemical carcass by the bleak magic of the barber's chair. In our anatomy of melancholy there are no such atrabiliar moments as those thirty-three (and a quarter) minutes once every ten weeks. Roughly speaking, we spend three hours of this living death every year.

And yet, perhaps it is worth it, for what a

Sitting in the Barber's Chair

jocund and pantheistic merriment possesses us when we escape from the shop! Bay-rummed, powdered, shorn, brisk and perfumed, we fare down the street exhaling the syrups of Cathay. Once more we can take our rightful place among aggressive and well-groomed men; we can look in the face without blenching those human leviathans who are ever creased, razored, and white-margined as to vest. We are a man among men and our untethered mind jostles the stars. We have had our hair cut, and no matter what gross contours our cropped skull may display to wives or ethnologists, we are a free man for ten dear weeks.

BROWN EYES AND EQUINOXES

W HAT is an equinox?" said Titania.

    I pretended not to hear her and prayed fervently that the inquiry would pass from her mind. Sometimes her questions, if ignored, are effaced by some other thought that possesses her active brain. I rattled my paper briskly and kept well behind it.

"Yes," I murmured husbandly, "delicious, delicious! My dear, you certainly plan the most delightful meals." Meanwhile I was glancing feverishly at the daily Quiz column to see if that noble cascade of popular information might give any help. It did not.

Clear brown eyes looked across the table gravely. I could feel them through the spring overcoat ads.

"What is an equinox?"

"I think I must have left my matches upstairs," I said, and went up to look for them. I stayed aloft ten minutes and hoped that by that time she would have passed on to some other topic. I did not waste my time, however; I looked everywhere for the "Children's Book

Brown Eyes and Equinoxes

of a Million Reasons," until I remembered it was under the dining-room table taking the place of a missing caster.

When I slunk into the living room again I hastily suggested a game of double Canfield, but Titania's brow was still perplexed. Looking across at me with that direct brown gaze that would compel even a milliner to relent, she asked:

"What is an equinox?"

I tried to pass it off flippantly.

"A kind of alarm clock," I said, "that lets the bulbs and bushes know it's time to get up."

"No; but honestly, Bob," she said, "I want to know. It's something about an equal day and an equal night, isn't it?"

"At the equinox," I said sternly, hoping to overawe her, "the day and the night are of equal duration. But only for one night. On the following day the sun, declining in perihelion, produces the customary inequality. The usual working day is much longer than the night of relaxation that follows it, as every toiler knows."

"Yes," she said thoughtfully, "but how does it work? It says something in this article about the days getting longer in the Northern Hemisphere, while they are getting shorter in the Southern."

Mince Pie

"Of course," I agreed, "conditions are totally different south of Mason and Dixon's line. But as far as we are concerned here, the sun, revolving round the earth, casts a beneficent shadow, which is generally regarded as the time to quit work. This shadow——"

"I thought the earth revolved round the sun," she said. "Wasn't that what Galileo proved?"

"He was afterward discovered to be mistaken," I said. "That was what caused all the trouble."

"What trouble?" she asked, much interested.

"Why, he and Socrates had to take hemlock or they were drowned in a butt of malmsey, I really forget which."

"Well, after the equinox," said Titania, "do the days get longer?"

"They do," I said; "in order to permit the double-headers. And now that daylight saving is to go into effect, equinoxes won't be necessary any more. Very likely the pan-Russian soviets, or President Wilson, or somebody, will abolish them."

"June 21 is the longest day in the year, isn't it?"

"The day before pay-day is always the longest day."

"And the night the cook goes out is always

the longest night," she retorted, catching the spirit of the game.

"Some day," I threatened her, "the earth will stop rotating on its orbit, or its axis, or whatever it is, and then we will be like the moon, divided into two hostile hemispheres, one perpetual day and the other eternal night."

She did not seem alarmed. "Yes, and I bet I know which one you'll emigrate to," she said. "But how about the equinoctial gales? Why should there be gales just then?"

I had forgot about the equinoctial gales, and this caught me unawares.

"That was an old tradition of the Phœnician mariners," I said, "but the invention of latitude and longitude made them unnecessary. They have fallen into disrepute. Dead reckoning killed them."

"And the precession of the equinoxes?" she asked, turning back to her magazine.

This was a poser, but I rallied stoutly. "Well," I said, "you see, there are two equinoxes a year, the vernal and the autumnal. They are well known by coal dealers. The first one is when he delivers the coal and the second is when he gets paid. Two of them a year, you see, in the course of a million years or so, makes quite a majestic series. That is why they call it a procession."

Mince Pie

Titania looked at me and gradually her face broke up into a charming aurora borealis of laughter.

"I don't believe you know any more about the old things than I do," she said.

And the worst of it is, I think she was right.

I FOUND Titania looking severely at her watch, which is a queer little gold disk about the size of a waistcoat button, swinging under her chin by a thin golden chain. Titania's methods of winding, setting and regulating that watch have always been a mystery to me. She frequently knows what the right time is, but how she deduces it from the data given by the hands of her timepiece I can't guess. It's something like this : She looks at the watch and notes what it says. Then she deducts ten minutes, because she remembers it is ten minutes fast. Then she performs some complicated calculation connected with when the baby had his bath, and how long ago she heard the church bells chime; to this result she adds five minutes to allow for leeway. Then she goes to the phone and asks Central the time.

"Hullo," I said; "what's wrong?"

"I'm wondering about this daylight-saving business," she said. "You know, I think it's all a piece of Bolshevik propaganda to get us

[69]

confused and encourage anarchy. All the women in Marathon are talking about it and neglecting their knitting. Junior's bath was half an hour late today because Mrs. Benvenuto called me up to talk about daylight saving. She says her cook has threatened to leave if she has to get up an hour earlier in the morning. I was just wondering how to adjust my watch to the new conditions."

"It's perfectly simple," I said. "Put your watch ahead one hour, and then go through the same logarithms you always do."

"Put it ahead?" asked Titania. "Mrs. Borgia says we have to put the clock *back* an hour. She is fearfully worried about it. She says suppose she has something in the oven when the clock is put back, it will be an hour overdone and burned to a crisp when the kitchen clock catches up again."

"Mrs. Borgia is wrong," I said. "The clocks are to be put ahead one hour. At 2 o'clock on Easter morning they are to be turned on to 3 o'clock. Mrs. Borgia certainly won't have anything in the oven at that time of night. You see, we are to pretend that 2 o'clock is really 3 o'clock, and when we get up at 7 o'clock it will really be 6 o'clock. We are deliberately fooling ourselves in order to get an hour more of daylight."

[70]

"I have an idea," she said, "that you won't get up at 7 that morning."

"It is quite possible," I said, "because I intend to stay up until 2 a. m. that morning in order to be exactly correct in changing our timepieces. No one shall accuse me of being a time slacker."

Titania was wrinkling her brow. "But how about that lost hour?" she said. "What happens to it? I don't see how we can just throw an hour away like that. Time goes on just the same. How can we afford to shorten our lives so ruthlessly? It's murder, that's what it is! I told you it was a Bolshevik plot. Just think; there are a hundred million Americans. Moving on the clock that way brings each of us one hour nearer our graves. That is to say, we are throwing away 100,000,000 hours."

She seized a pencil and a sheet of paper and went through some calculations.

"There are 8,760 hours in a year," she said, "Reckoning seventy years a lifetime, there are 613,200 hours in each person's life. Now, will you please divide that into a hundred million for me? I'm not good at long division."

With docility I did so, and reported the result.

"About 163," I said.

"There you are!" she exclaimed triumphant-

ly. "Throwing away all that perfectly good
time amounts simply to murdering 163 harm-
less old men of seventy, or 326 able-bodied men
of thirty-five, or 1,630 innocent little children
of seven. If that isn't atrocity, what is? I
think Mr. Hoover or Admiral Grayson, or somebody, ought to be prosecuted."

I was aghast at this awful result. Then an
idea struck me, and I took the pencil and began to figure on my own account.

"Look here, Titania," I said. "Not so fast.
Moving the clock ahead doesn't really bring
those people any nearer their graves. What it
does do is bring the ratification of the Peace
Treaty sooner, which is a fine thing. By de-
leting a hundred million hours we shorten Sena-
tor Borah's speeches against the League by
11,410 years. That's very encouraging."

"According to that way of reckoning," she
said with sarcasm, "Mr. Borah's term must
have expired about 11,000 years ago."

"My dear Titania," I said, "the ways of the
Government may seem inscrutable, but we have
got to follow them with faith. If Mr. Wilson
tells us to murder 163 fine old men in elastic-
sided boots we must simply do it, that's all.
Peace is a dreadful thing. We have got to meet
the Germans on their own ground. They
adopted this daylight-saving measure years ago.

[72]

They call it Sonnenuntergangverderbenpraxis, I believe. After all, it is only a temporary measure, because in the fall, when the daylight hours get shorter, we shall have to turn the clocks back a couple of hours in order to compensate the gas and electric light companies for all the money they will have lost. That will bring those 163 old gentlemen to life again and double their remaining term of years to make up for their temporary effacement. They are patriotic hostages to Time for the summer only. You must remember that time is only a philosophical abstraction, with no real or tangible existence, and we have a right to do whatever we want with it."

"I will remind you of that," she said, "at getting-up time on Sunday morning. I still think that if we are going to monkey with the clocks at all it would be better to turn them backward instead of forward. Certainly that would bring you home from the club a little earlier."

"My dear," I said, "we are in the Government's hands. A little later we may be put on time rations, just as we are on food rations. We may have time cards to encourage thrift in saving time. Every time we save an hour we will get a little stamp to show for it. When we fill out a whole card we will be entitled to call

ourselves a month younger than we are. Tell
that to Mrs. Borgia; it will reconcile her."

A lusty uproar made itself heard upstairs,
and Titania gave a little scream. "Heavens!" she
cried. "Here I am talking with you and Junior's bottle is half an hour late. I don't care
what Mr. Wilson does to the clocks; he won't
be able to fool Junior. He knows when it's
time for meals. Won't you call up Central
and find out the exact time?"

A TRAGIC SMELL IN MARATHON

Marathon, Pa., April 2.

THIS is a very embarrassing time of year for us. Every morning when we get on the 8:13 train at Marathon Bill Stites or Fred Myers or Hank Harris or some other groundsel philosopher on the Cinder and Bloodshot begins to chivvy us about our garden. "Have you planted anything yet?" they say. "Have you put litmus paper in the soil to test it for lime, potash and phosphorus? Have you got a harrow?"

That sort of thing bothers us, because our ideas of cultivation are very primitive. We did go to the newsstand at the Reading Terminal and try to buy a Litmus paper, but the agent didn't have any. He says he doesn't carry the Jersey papers. So we buried some old copies of the *Philistine* in the garden, thinking that would strengthen up the soil a bit. This business of nourishing the soil seems grotesque. It's hard enough to feed the family, let alone throwing away good money on feeding the land. Our idea about soil is that it ought to feed itself.

[75]

Mince Pie

Our garden ought to be lusty enough to raise the few beans and beets and blisters we aspire to. We have been out looking at the soil. It looks fairly potent and certainly it goes a long way down. There are quite a lot of broken magnesia bottles and old shinbones scattered through it, and they ought to help along. The topsoil and the humus may be a little mixed, but we are not going to sort them out by hand.

Our method is to go out at twilight the first Sunday in April, about the time the cutworms go to roost, and take a sharp-pointed stick. We draw lines in the ground with this stick, preferably in a pleasant geometrical pattern that will confuse the birds and other observers. It is important not to do this until twilight, so that no robins or insects can watch you. Then we go back in the house and put on our old trousers, the pair that has holes in each pocket. We fill the pockets with the seed we want to plant and loiter slowly along the grooves we have made in the earth. The seed sifts down the trousers legs and spreads itself in the furrow far better than any mechanical drill could do it. The secret of gardening is to stick to nature's old appointed ways. Then we read a chapter of Bernard Shaw aloud, by candle light or lantern light. As soon as they hear the voice of Shaw all the vegetables dig

themselves in. This saves going all along the
rows with a shingle to pat down the topsoil
or the humus or the magnesia bottles or whatever else is uppermost.

Fred says that certain vegetables—kohl-rabi
and colanders, we think—extract nitrogen from
the air and give it back to the soil. It may
be so, but what has that to do with us? If
our soil can't keep itself supplied with nitro-

gen, that's its lookout. We don't need the
nitrogen in the air. The baby isn't old enough
to have warts yet.

Hank says it's no use watering the garden
from above. He says that watering from above
lures the roots toward the surface and next
day the hot sun kills them. The answer to
that is that the rain comes from above, doesn't
it? Roots have learned certain habits in the
past million years and we haven't time to teach
them to duck when it rains. Hank has some

irrigation plan which involves sinking tomato cans in the ground and filling them with water.

Bill says it's dangerous to put arsenic on the plants, because it may kill the cook. He says nicotine or tobacco dust is far better. The answer to that is that we never put fertilizers on our garden, anyway. If we want to kill the cook there is a more direct method, and we reserve the tobacco for ourself. No cutworm shall get a blighty one from our cherished baccy pouch.

Fred says we ought to have a wheel-barrow; Hank swears by a mulching iron; Bill is all for cold frames. All three say that hellebore is the best thing for sucking insects. We echo the expletive, with a different application.

You see, we have no instinct for gardening. Some fellows, like Bill Stites, have a divinely implanted zest for the propagation of chard and rhubarb and self-blanching celery and kohl-rabi; they are kohl-rabid, we might say. They know just what to do when they see a weed; they can assassinate a weevil by just looking at it. But weevils and cabbage worms are unterrified by us. We can't tell a weed from a young onion. We never mulched any-

[78]

A Tragic Smell in Marathon

thing in our life; we wouldn't know how to begin.

But the deuce of it is, public opinion says that we must raise a garden. It is no use to hire a man to do it for us. However badly we may do it, patriotism demands that we monkey around with a garden of our own. We may get bitten by a snapping bean or routed by a rutabaga or infected by a parsnip. But with Bill and those fellows at our heels we have just got to face it. Hellebore!

What we want to know is, How do you ever find out all these things about vegetables? We bought an ounce of tomato seeds in desperation, and now Fred says "one ounce of tomato seeds will produce 3,000 plants. You should have bought two dozen plants instead of the seed." How does he know those things? Hank says beans are very delicate and must not be handled while they are wet or they may get rusty. Again we ask, how does he know? Where do they learn these matters? Bill says that stones draw out the moisture from the soil and every stone in the garden should be removed by hand before we plant. We offered him twenty cents an hour to do it.

The most tragic odor in the world hangs over Marathon these days; the smell of freshly spaded earth. It is extolled by the poets and all those happy sons of the pavement who know nothing about it. But here are we, who hardly know a loam from a lentil, breaking our back over seed catalogues. Public opinion may compel us to raise vegetables, but we are going to go about it our own way. If the stones are going to act like werewolves and suck the moisture from our soil, let them do so. We don't believe in thwarting nature. Maybe it will be a very wet summer and we shall have the laugh on Bill, who has carted away all his stones.

And we should just like to see Bill Stites write a poem. We bet it wouldn't look as much like a poem as our beans look like beans. And as for Hank and Fred, they wouldn't even know how to begin to plant a poem!

BULLIED BY THE BIRDS

Marathon, Pa., May 2.

I INSIST that the place for birds is in the air or on the bushy tops of trees or on smooth-shaven lawns. Let them twitter and strut on the greens of golf courses and intimidate the tired business men. Let them peck cinders along the railroad track and keep the trains waiting. But really they have no right to take possession of a man's house as they have mine.

The nesting season is a time of tyranny and oppression for those who live in Marathon. The birds are upon us like Hindenburg in Belgium. We go about on tiptoe, speaking in whispers, for fear of annoying them. It is all the fault of the Marathon Bird Club, which has offered all sorts of inducements to the fowls of the air to come and live in our suburb, quite forgetting that humble commuters have to live there, too. Birds have moved all the way from Wynnewood and Ambler and Chestnut Hill to enjoy the congenial air of Marathon and the informing little pamphlets of our club,

Mince Pie

telling them just what to eat and which houses offer the best hospitality. All our dwellings are girt about with little villas made of condensed milk boxes, but the feathered tyrants have grown too pernickety to inhabit these. They come closer still, and make our homes their own. They take the grossest liberties.

I am fond of birds, but I think the line must be drawn somewhere. The clothes-line, for instance. The other day Titania sent me out to put up a new clothesline; I found that a shrike or a barn swallow or some other veery had built a nest in the clothespin basket. That means we won't be able to hang out our laundry in the fresh Monday air and equally fresh Monday sunshine until the nesting season is over.

Then there is a gross, fat, indiscreet robin that has taken a home in an evergreen or mimosa or banyan tree just under our veranda railing. It is an absurdly exposed, almost indecently exposed position, for the confidential family business she intends to carry on. The iceman and the butcher and the boy who brings up the Sunday ice cream from the apothecary can't help seeing those three big blue eggs she has laid. But, because she has nested there for the last three springs, while the use was unoccupied, she thinks she has a perpetual lease on that bush. She hotly resents the iceman and the butcher and the apothecary's boy, to say nothing of me. So these worthy merchants have to trail round a circuitous route, violating the neutral ground of a neighbor, in order to reach the house from behind and deliver their wares through the cellar. We none of us dare use the veranda

at all for fear of frightening her, and I have given up having the morning paper delivered at the house because she made such shrill protest.

Frightening her, do I say? Nay, it is *we* who are frightened. I go round to the side of the house to prune my benzine bushes or to plant a mess of spinach and a profane starling or woodpecker bustles off her nest with shrewish outcry and lingers nearby to rail

[83]

at me. Abashed, I stealthily scuffle back to get a spade out of the tool bin and again that shrill scream of anger and outraged motherhood. A throstle or a whippoorwill is raising a family in the gutter spout over the back kitchen. I go into the bathroom to shave and Titania whispers sharply, "You mustn't shave in there. There's a tomtit nesting in the shutter hinge and the light from your shaving mirror will make the poor little birds crosseyed when they're hatched." I try to shave in the dining-room and I find a sparrow's nest on the window sill. Finally I do my toilet in the coal bin, even though there is a young squeaking bat down there. A bat is half mouse anyway, so Titania has less compassion for its feelings. Even if that bat grows up bow-legged on account of premature excitement, I have to shave somewhere.

We can't play croquet at this time of year, because the lawn must be kept clear for the robins to quarry out worms. The sound of mallet and ball frightens the worms and sends them underground, and then it's harder for the robins to find them. I suppose we really ought to keep a stringed orchestra playing in the garden to entice the worms to the surface. We have given up frying onions because the mother robins don't like the odor while they're

Bullied by the Birds

raising a family. I love my toast crusts, but
Titania takes them away from me for the
blackbirds. "Now," she says, "they're raising
a family. You must be generous."

If my garden doesn't amount to anything
this year the birds will be my alibi. Titania
makes me do my gardening in rubber-soled
shoes so as not to disturb the birds when they
are going to bed. (They begin yelping at 4
a. m. right outside the window and never think
of my slumbers.) The other evening I put
on my planting trousers and was about to sow
a specially fine pea I had brought home from
town when Titania made signs from the window. "You simply mustn't wear those trousers
around the house in nesting season. Don't you
know the birds are very sensitive just now?"
And we have been paying board for our cat on
Long Island for a whole year because the birds
wouldn't like his society and plebeian ways.

Marathon has come to a pretty pass, indeed,
when the commuters are to be dispossessed in
this way by a lot of birds, orioles and tom-
tits and yellow-bellied nuthatches. Some of
these days a wren will take it into its head to
build a nest on the railroad track and we'll
all have to walk to town. Or a chicken hawk
will settle in our icebox and we'll starve to
death.

[85]

Mince Pie

As I have said before, I believe in keeping nature in its proper place. Birds belong in trees. I don't go twittering and fluffing about in oaks and chestnuts, perching on the birds' nest steps and getting in their way. And why should some swarthy robin, be she never so matronly, swear at me if I set foot on my own front porch?

A MESSAGE FOR BOONVILLE

WHEN corncob pipes went up from a nickel to six cents, smoking traditions tottered. That was a year or more ago, but one can still recall the indignation written on the faces of nicotine-soaked gaffers who had been buying cobs at a jitney ever since Washington used one to keep warm at Valley Forge. It was the supreme test of our determination to win the war: the price of Missouri meerschaums went up 20 per cent and there was no insurrection.

Yesterday we went out to buy our annual corncob, and were agreeably surprised to learn that the price is still six cents; but our friend the tobacconist said that it may go up again soon. We took the treasure, gleaming yellow with fresh varnish, back to our kennel, and we are smoking it as we set down these words. A corncob is sadly hot and raw until it is well sooted, but the ultimate flavor is worth persecution.

The corncob pipes we always buy come from Boonville, Mo., and we don't see why we shouldn't blow a little whiff of affection and

[87]

Mince Pie

gratitude toward that excellent town. Moreover, Boonville celebrated its centennial recently: it was founded in 1818. If the map is
to be believed, it is on the southern bank of
the Missouri River, which is there spanned by
a very fine bridge; it is reached by two rail-
roads (Missouri Pacific and M., K. and T.) and
stands on a bluff 100 feet above the water. According to the two works of reference nearest
to our desk, its population is either 4252 or
4377. Perhaps the former census omits the
125 men of the town who are so benighted as
to smoke briars or clays.

Delightful town of Boonville, seat of Cooper
County, you are well named. How great a
boon you have conferred upon a troubled world!
Long after more ambitious towns have faded
in the memory of man your quiet and soothing
gift to humanity will make your name blessed.
I like to imagine your shady streets, drows-
ing in the summer sun, and the rural philoso-
phers sitting on the verandas of your hotels or
on the benches of Harley Park ("comprising
fifteen acres"—New International Encyclo-
pedia), looking out across the brown river and
puffing clouds of sweet gray reek. Down by
the livery stable on Main street (there must
be a livery stable on Main street) I can see the
old creaky, cane-bottomed chairs (with seats

punctured by too much philosophy) tilted against the sycamore trees, ready for the afternoon gossip and shag tobacco. I can imagine the small boys of Boonville fishing for catfish from the piers of the bridge or bathing down by the steamboat dock (if there is one), and yearning for the day when they, too, will be grown up and old enough to smoke corncobs.

What is the subtle magic of a corncob pipe?

It is never as sweet or as mellow as a well-seasoned briar, and yet it has a fascination all its own. It is equally dear to those who work hard and those who loaf with intensity. When you put your nose to the blackened mouth of the hot cob its odor is quite different from that fragrance of the crusted wooden bowl. There is a faint bitterness in it, a sour, plaintive aroma. It is a pipe that seems to call aloud for the accompaniment of beer and earnest argument on factional political matters. It is

[89]

Mince Pie

also the pipe for solitary vigils of hard and concentrated work. It is the pipe that a man keeps in the drawer of his desk for savage hours of extra toil after the stenographer has powdered her nose and gone home.

A corncob pipe is a humble badge of philosophy, an evidence of tolerance and even humor. It requires patience and good cheer, for it is slow to "break in." Those who meditate bestial and brutal designs against the weak and innocent do not smoke it. Probably Hindenburg never saw one. Missouri's reputation for incredulity may be due to the corncob habit. One who is accustomed to consider an argument over a burning nest of tobacco, with the smoke fuming upward in a placid haze, will not accept any dogma too immediately.

There is a singular affinity among those who smoke corncobs. A Missouri meerschaum whose bowl is browned and whose fiber stem is frayed and stringy with biting betrays a meditative and reasonable owner. He will have pondered all aspects of life and be equally ready to denounce any of them, but without bitterness. If you see a man on a street corner smoking a cob it will be safe to ask him to watch the baby a minute while you slip around the corner. You would even be safe in asking

[90]

A Message for Boonville

him to lend you a five. He will be safe, too,
because he won't have it.

Think, therefore, of the charm of a town
where corncob pipes are the chief industry.
Think of them stacked up in bright yellow
piles in the warehouse. Think of the warm
sun and the wholesome sweetness of broad acres
that have grown into the pith of the cob. Think
of the bright-eyed Missouri maidens who have
turned and scooped and varnished and packed
them. Think of the airy streets and wide pavements of Boonville, and the corner drug stores
with their shining soda fountains and grape-
juice bottles. Think of sitting out on that
bluff on a warm evening, watching the broad
shimmer of the river slipping down from the
sunset, and smoking a serene pipe while the
local flappers walk in the coolness wearing
crisp, swaying gingham dresses. That's the
kind of town we like to think about.

MAKING MARATHON SAFE FOR THE URCHIN

THE Urchin and I have been strolling about Marathon on Sunday mornings for more than a year, but not until the gasolineless Sabbaths supervened were we really able to examine the village and see what it is like. Previously we had been kept busy either dodging motors or admiring them as they sped by. Their rich dazzle of burnished enamel, the purring hum of their great tires, evokes applause from the Urchin. He is learning, as he watches those flashing chariots, that life truly is almost as vivid as the advertisements in the *Ladies' Home Journal,* where the shimmer of earthly pageant first was presented to him.

Marathon is a village so genteel and comely that the Urchin and I would like to have some pictures of it for future generations, particularly as we see it on an autumn morning when, as I say, the motors are kenneled and the landscape has ceased to vibrate. In the douce benignance of equinoctial sunshine we gaze about

[92]

Making Marathon Safe for the Urchin

us with eyes of inventory. Where my observation errs by too much sentiment the Urchin checks me by his cooler power of ratiocination.

Marathon is a suburban Xanadu gently caressed by the train service of the Cinder and Bloodshot. It may be recognized as an aristocratic and patrician stronghold by the fact that while luxuries are readily obtainable (for instance, banana splits, or the latest novel by Enoch A. Bennett), necessaries are had only by prayer and advowson. The drug store will deliver ice cream to your very refrigerator, but it is impossible to get your garbage collected. The cook goes off for her Thursday evening in a taxi, but you will have to mend the roof, stanch the plumbing and curry the furnace with your own hands. There are ten trains to take you to town of an evening, but only two to bring you home. Yet going to town is a luxury, coming home is a necessity. The supply of grape juice seems almost unlimited, yet coal is to be had catch-as-catch-can.

Another proof that Marathon is patrician at heart is that nothing is known by its right name! The drug store is a "pharmacy," Sunday is "the Sabbath," a house is a "residence," a debt is a "balance due on bill rendered." A girls' school is a "young ladies' seminary." A Marathon man is not drafted, he is "inducted

[93]

into selective service." And the railway station has a porte cochère (with the correct accent) instead of a carriage entrance. A furnace is (how erroneously!) called a "heater." Marathon people do not die—they "pass away." Even the cobbler, good fellow, has caught the trick; he calls his shop the "Italo-American Shoe Hospital."

This is an innocent masquerade! If Marathon prefers not to call a flivver a flivver, I shall not expostulate. And yet this quaint subterfuge should not be carried quite so far. Stone walls are made for sunny lounging; yet stone walls in Marathon are built with uneven vertical projections to discourage the sedentary. Nothing is more delightful than a dog; but there are no dogs in Marathon. They are all airedales or spaniels or mastiffs. If an ordinary dog should wag his tail up our street the airedales would cut him dead. Bless me, Nature herself has taken to the same insincerity. The landscape round Marathon is lovely, but it has itself well in hand. The hills all pretend to be gentle declivities. There is a beautiful little sheet of water, reflecting the trailery of willows, a green salute to the eye. In a robuster community it would be a swimming hole—but with us, an ornamental lake! Only in one spot has Nature forgotten her-

self and been so brusque and rough as to
jut up a very sizable cliff. This is the loveliest
thing in Marathon: sunlight and shadow break
and angle in cubist magnificence among the
oddly veined knobs and prisms of brown stone.
Yet this cliff or quarry is by common consent
taboo among us. It is our indelicacy, our in-
decency. Such "residences" as are near modestly turn their kitchens toward it. Only the
blacksmith and the gas tanks are hardy enough
to face this nakedness of Mother Earth—they,
and excellent Pat Lemon, Marathon's humblest
and blackest citizen, who contemplates that
rugged and honest beauty as he tills his garden on the land abandoned by squeamish burgh-
ers. That is our Aceldama, our Potter's Field,
only approached by the athletic, who keep their
eyes from Nature's indiscretion by vigorous sets
of tennis in the purple shadow of the cliff.

Life is queerly inverted in Marathon. Nature has been so bullied and repressed that she
fawns about us timidly. No well-conducted
suburban shrubbery would think of assuming
autumn tints before the ladies have got into
their fall fashions. Indeed none of our chaste
trees will even shed their leaves while any one
is watching; and they crouch modestly in the
shade of our massive garages. They have been
taught their place. In Marathon it is a worse

sin to have your lawn uncut than to have your
books or your hair uncut. I have been aware
of indignant eyes because I let my back garden run wild. And yet I flatter myself it was
not mere sloth. No! I want the Urchin to
see what this savage, tempestuous world is like.
What preparation for life is a village where
Nature comes to heel like a spaniel? When a
thunderstorm disorganizes our electric lights
for an hour or so we feel it a personal affront.
Let my rearward plot be a deep-tangled wild-
wood where the happy Urchin may imagine
something more ferocious lurking than a posse
of radishes. Indeed, I hardly know whether
Marathon is a safe place to bring up a child.
How can he learn the horrors of drink in a village where there is no saloon? Or the sadness
of the seven deadly sins where there is no
movie? Or deference to his betters where the
chauffeurs, in their withered leather legs, drive
limousines to the drug store to buy expensive
cigars, while their employers walk to the station puffing briar pipes?

I had been hoping that the war would knock
some of this topsy-turvy nonsense out of us.
Maybe it has. Sometimes I see on the faces
of our commuters the unaccustomed agitation
of thought. At least we still have the grace
to call ourselves a suburb, and not (what we

fancy ourselves) a superurb. But I don't like the pretense that runs like a jarring note through the music of our life. Why is it that those who are doing the work must pretend they are not doing it; and those not doing the work pretend that they are? I see that the motor messenger girls who drive high-powered cars wear Sam Browne belts and heavy-soled boots, whereas the stalwart colored wenches who labor along the tracks of the Cinder and Bloodshot console themselves with flimsy waists and light slippers. (A fact!) By and by the Urchin will notice these things. And I don't want him to grow up the kind of chap who, instead of running to catch a train, loiters gracefully to the station and waits to be caught.

THE SMELL OF SMELLS

I SMELT it this morning—I wonder if you know the smell I mean?

It had rained hard during the night, and trees and bushes twinkled in the sharp early sunshine like ballroom chandeliers. As soon as I stepped out of doors I caught that faint but unmistakable musk in the air; that dim, warm sweetness. It was the smell of summer, so wholly different from the crisp tang of spring.

It is a drowsy, magical waft of warmth and fragrance. It comes only when the leaves and vegetation have grown to a certain fullness and juice, and when the sun bends in his orbit near enough to draw out all the subtle vapors of field and woodland. It is a smell that rarely if ever can be discerned in the city. It needs the wider air of the unhampered earth for its circulation and play.

I don't know just why, but I associate that peculiar aroma of summer with woodpiles and barnyards. Perhaps because in the area of a farmyard the sunlight is caught and focused and glows with its fullest heat and radiance. And it is in the grasp of the relentless sun that growing things yield up their innermost vitality and emanate their fragrant essence. I have seen fields of tobacco under a hot sun that smelt as blithe as a room thick with blue Havana smoke. I remember a pile of birch logs, heaped up behind a barn in Pike County, where

that mellow richness of summer flowed and quivered like a visible exhalation in the air. It is the goodly soul of earth, rendering her health and sweetness to her master, the sun.

Every one, I suppose, who is a fancier of smells, knows this blithe perfume of the summer air that is so pleasant to the nostril almost any fine forenoon from mid-June until August. It steals pungently through the blue sparkle of the morning, fading away toward noon when the moistness is dried out. But when one first

[99]

issues from the house at breakfast time it is at its highest savor. Irresistibly it suggests worms, and a tin can with the lid jaggedly bent back, and a pitchfork turning up the earth behind the cow stable. Fishing was first invented when Adam smelt that odor in the air.

The first fishing morning—can't you imagine it! Has no one ever celebrated it in verse or oils? The world all young and full of unmitigated sweetness; the Garden of Eden bespangled with the early dew; Adam scrabbling up a fistful of worms and hooking them on a bent thorn and a line of twisted pampas grass; hurrying down to the branch or the creek or the bayou or whatever it may have been; sitting down on a brand-new stump that the devil had put there to tempt him; throwing out his line; sitting there in the sun dreaming and brooding. . . .

And then a tug, a twitch, a flurry in the clear water of Eden, a pull, a splash, and the First Fish lay on the grass at Adam's foot. Can you imagine his sensations? How he yelled to Eve to come—look—see, and how annoyed he was because she called out she was busy. . . .

Probably it was in that moment that all the bickerings and back-talk of husbands and wives originated; when Adam called to Eve to come and look at his First Fish while it was still sil-

The Smell of Smells

ver and vivid in its living colors; and Eve answered she was busy. In that moment were born the men's clubs and the women's clubs and the pinochle parties and being detained at the office and Kelly pool and all the other devices and stratagems that keep men and women from taking their amusements together.

Well, I didn't mean to go back to the Garden of Eden; I just wanted to say that summer is here again, even though the almanac doesn't vouch for it until the 21st. Those of you who are fond of smells, spread your nostrils about breakfast time tomorrow morning and see if you detect it.

A JAPANESE BACHELOR

THE first obligation of one who lives by writing is to write what editors will buy. In so doing, how often one laments that one cannot write exactly what happens. Suppose I were to try it—for once!

I have been lying on the bed—where the landlady has put a dark blue spread, instead of the white one, because I drop my tobacco ashes—smoking, and thinking about a new friend I met today. His name is Kenko, a Japanese bachelor of the fourteenth century, who wrote a little book of musings which has been translated under the title "The Miscellany of a Japanese Priest." His candid reflections are those of a shrewd, learned, humane and somewhat misogynist mind. I have been lying on the bed because his book, like all books that make one ponder deeply on human destiny, causes that feeling of mind-sickness, that swimming pain of the mental faculties—or is it caused by too much strong tobacco?

My acquaintance with Kenko began only last night, when I sat in bed reading Mr. Raymond

A Japanese Bachelor

Weaver's very pleasant article about him in a recent *Bookman*. My last act before turning out the light was to lay the magazine on the table, open at Mr. Weaver's essay, to remind me to get a copy of Kenko the first thing this morning. Happily to-day was Saturday. I don't know what I should have done if it had been Sunday. I felt that I could not wait another day without owning that book. I suspected it was a good deal in the mood of another bachelor, an Anglo-American Caleb of to-day—Mr. Logan Pearsall Smith, whose whimsical "Trivia" belongs on the same shelf.

This morning I tried to argue myself out of the decision. It may be a very expensive book, I thought; it may cost two or three dollars; I have been spending a lot of money lately, and I certainly ought to buy some new undershirts. Moreover, this has been a bad week; I have never written those paragraphs I promised a certain editor, and I haven't paid the rent yet. Why not try to find the book at a library? But I knew the only library where I would have any chance of finding Kenko would be the big pile at Fifth avenue and Forty-second street, and I could not bear the thought of having to read that book without smoking. I felt instinctively (from what Mr.

Weaver had written) that it was the kind of book that requires a pipe.

Well, I thought, I won't decide this too hastily; I'll walk down to the post office (four blocks) and make up my mind on the way. I knew already, however, that if I didn't go downtown for that book it would bother me all day and ruin my work.

I walked down to the post office (to mail to an editor a sonnet I thought fairly well of) saying to myself: That book is imported from England, it may be a big book, it may even cost four dollars. How much better to exhibit the stoic tenacity of all great men, go back to my hall bedroom (which I was temporarily occupying) and concentrate on matters in hand. What right, I said, has a Buddhist recluse, born either in 1281 or 1283, to harass me so? But I knew in my heart that the matter was already decided. I walked back to the corner of Hall-bedroom street, and stood vacillating at the newsstand, pretending to glance over the papers. But across six centuries the insistent ghost of Kenko had me in its grip. Annoyed, and with a sense of chagrin, I hurried to the subway.

In the dimly lit vestibule of the subway car, a boy of sixteen or so sat on an up-ended suitcase, plunged in a book. I can never resist the temptation to try to see what books other people are reading. This innocent curiosity has led me into many rudenesses, for I am short-sighted and have to stare very close to make out the titles. And usually the people who read books on trolleys, subways and ferries are women. How often I have stalked them warily, trying to identify the volume without seeming too intrusive. That weakness deserves an essay in itself. It has led me into surprising adventures. But in this case my quarry was easy. The lad—I judged him a boarding school boy going back to school after the holidays—was so absorbed in his reading that it was easy to thrust my face over his shoulder and see the running head on the page— "The Light That Failed."

I left the subway at Pennsylvania Station. Just to appease my conscience, I stopped in at the agreeable Cadmus bookshop on Thirty-third street to see if by any chance they might have a second-hand copy of Kenko. But I know they wouldn't; it is not the kind of book at all likely to be found second-hand. I tarried here long enough to smoke one cigarette and pay my devoirs to the noble profession of second-hand bookselling. I even thought, a little wildly, of buying a copy of "The Monk" by M. G. Lewis, which I saw there. So does the frenzy

Mince Pie

rage when once you unleash it. But I decided
to be content with paying my devoirs to the
proprietor, a friend of mine, and not go on (as
the soldier does in Hood's lovely pun) to de-
vour my pay. I hurried off to the office of the
Oxford University Press, Kenko's publishers.

It should be stated, however, that owing to
some confusion of doors I got by mistake into
the reception room of the Brunswick-Balke-
Collender Billiard Table Company, which is on
the same corridor as the salesroom of the Oxford Press. It was a pleasant reception room,
not very bookish in aspect, but in my agitation
I was too eager to feel surprised by the large
billiard table in the offing. I somewhat star-
tled a young man at an adding machine by de-
manding, in a husky voice, a copy of "The
Miscellanies of a Japanese Priest." I was
rather nervous by this time, lest for some reason I should not be able to buy a copy of Kenko.
I feared the publishers might be angry with
me for not having made a round of the book-
stores first. The young man saw that I was
chalking the wrong cue, and forwarded me.

In the office of the Oxford Press I met a
very genial reception. I had been, as I say, ap-
prehensive lest they should refuse to sell me
the book; or perhaps they might not have a
copy. I wondered what credentials I could of-

fer to override their scruples. I had made up my mind to tell them, if they demurred, that I had once published an essay to prove that the best book for reading in bed is the General Catalogue of the Oxford University Press. This is quite true. It is a delightful compilation of several thousand pages, on India paper. But to my pleasant surprise the Oxonians seemed not at all surprised at the sudden appearance of one asking, in a voice a little shaken with emotion, for a copy of the "Miscellanies." Mr. Campion and Mr. Krause, who greeted me, were kindness itself.

"Oh, yes," they said, "we have a copy." And in a minute it lay before me. One of those little green and gold volumes in the Oxford Library of Prose and Poetry. "How much?" I said. "A dollar forty." I paid it joyfully. It is a good price for a book. Once I wrote a book myself that sells (when it does sell) at that figure. When I was at Oxford I used to buy the O. L. P. P. books for (I think) half a crown. In 1917 they were listed at a dollar. Now $1.40. But I fear Kenko's estate doesn't get the advantage of increased royalties.

The first thing to do was to find a place to read the book. My club was fifteen blocks away. The smoking room of the Pennsylvania Station, where I have done much reading, was three

Mince Pie

long blocks. But I must dip into Kenko immediately. Down in the hallway I found a
shoe-shining stand, with a bowl of indirect light
above it. The artist was busy in the barber
shop near-by. Admirable opportunity. I
mounted the throne and fell to. The first thing
I saw was a quaint Japanese woodcut of a
buxom maiden washing garments in a rapidly
purling stream. She was treading out a pet-
ticoat with her bare feet, presumably on a flat
stone. In a black storm-cloud above a willow
tree a bearded supernatural being, with hands
spread in humorous deprecation, gazes down
half pleased, half horrified. And the caption is,
"Did not the fairy Kumé lose his supernatural
powers when he saw the white legs of a girl
washing clothes?" Yet be not dismayed. Kenko is no George Moore.

By and bye the shoeshiner came out and
found me reading. He was apologetic. "I
didn't know you were here," he said. "Sorry
to keep you waiting." Fortunately my shoes
needed shining, as they generally do. He
shined them, and I still sat reading. He was
puzzled, and tried to make out the title of the
book. At that moment I was reading:

One morning after a beautiful snowfall I sent a
letter to a friend's house about something I wished

A Japanese Bachelor

to say, but said nothing at all about the snow. And in his reply he wrote: "How can I listen to a man so base that his pen in writing did not make the least reference to the snow! Your honorable way of expressing yourself I exceedingly regret." How amusing was this answer!

The shoeshiner was now asking me whether anything was wrong with the polish he had put on my boots, so I thought it best to leave.

In the earlier pages of Kenko's book there are a number of allusions to the agreeableness of intercourse with friends, so I went into a nearby restaurant to telephone to a man whom I wished to know better. He said that he would be happy to meet me at ten minutes after twelve. That left over half an hour. I felt an immediate necessity to tell some one about Kenko, so I made my way to Mr. Nichols's delightful bookshop (which has an open fire) on Thirty-third Street. I showed the book to Mr. Nichols, and we had a pleasant talk, in the course of which she showed me the five facsimile volumes of Dickens's Christmas books, which he had issued. In particular, he read aloud to me the magnificent description of the boiling kettle in the first "Chirp" of "The Cricket on the Hearth," and pointed out to me how Dickens fell into rhyme in describing the song of the kettle. This passage Mr. Nichols read to me, standing in front of his fire, in a very musical and sympathetic tone of voice, which pleased me exceedingly. I was strongly tempted to buy the five little books, and wished I had known of them before Christmas. With a brutal effort at last I pulled out my watch, and found it was a quarter after twelve.

I met my friend at his office, and we walked up Fourth Avenue in a flush of sunshine. From Twenty-fourth to Forty-second Street we discussed the habits of English poets visiting this country. At the club we got onto Bolshevism, and he told me how a bookseller on Lexington Avenue, whose shop is frequented by very outspoken radicals, had told him that one of these had said, "The time is coming, and not far away, when the gutters in front of your shop will run with blood as they did in Petrograd." I thought of some recent bomb outrages in Philadelphia and did not laugh. With such current problems before us, I felt a little embarrassed about turning the talk back to so many centuries to Kenko, but finally I got it there. My friend ate chicken hash and tea; I had kidneys and bacon, and cocoa with whipped cream. We both had a coffee éclair. We parted with mutual regret, and I went back to the Hall-bedroom street, intending to do some work.

A Japanese Bachelor

Of course you know that I didn't do it. I lit the gas stove, and sat down to read Kenko. I wished I were a recluse, living somewhere near a plum tree and a clear running water, leisurely penning maxims for posterity. I read about his frugality, his love of the moon and a little music, his somewhat embittered complaints against the folly of men who spend their lives in rushing about swamped in petty affairs, and the sad story of the old priest who was attacked by a goblin-cat when he came home late at night from a pleasant evening spent in capping verses. I read with special pleasure his seven Self-Congratulations, in which he records seven occasions when he felt that he had really done himself justice. The first of these was when he watched a man riding horseback in a reckless fashion; he predicted that the man would come a cropper, and he did so. The next four self-congratulations refer to times when his knowledge of literary and artistic matters enabled him to place an unfamiliar quotation or assign a painted tablet to the right artist. One tells how he was able to find a man in a crowd when everyone else had failed. And the last and most amusing is an anecdote of a court lady who tried to inveigle him into a flirtation with her maid by sending the latter, richly dressed and perfumed, to sit

[111]

very close to him when he was at the temple. Kenko congratulates himself on having been adamant. He was no Pepys.

I thought of trying to set down a similar list of self-congratulations for myself. Alas, the only two I could think of were having remembered a telephone number, the memorandum of which I had lost; and having persuaded a publisher to issue a novel which was a great success. (Not written by me, let me add.)

I found my friend Kenko a rather disturbing companion. His condemnation of our busy, racketing life is so damned conclusive! Having recently added to my family, I was distressed by his section "Against Leaving Any Descendants." He seems to be devoid of the sentiment of ancestor worship and sacredness of family continuity which we have been taught to associate with the Oriental. And yet there is always a current of suspicion in one's mind that he is not really revealing his inmost heart. When a bachelor in his late fifties tells us how glad he is never to have had a son, we begin to taste sour grapes.

I went out about six o'clock, and was thrilled by a shaving of shining new moon in the cold blue winter sky—"the sky with its terribly cold clear moon, which none care to watch, is simply heart-breaking," says Kenko. As I walked up Broadway I turned back for another look at the moon, and found it hidden by the vast bulk of a hotel. Kenko would have had some caustic remark for that. I went into the Milwaukee Lunch for supper. They had just baked some of their delicious fresh bran muffins, still hot from the oven. I had two of them, sliced and buttered, with a pot of tea. Kenko lay on the table, and the red-headed philosopher who runs the lunchroom spotted him. I have always noticed that "plain men" are vastly curious about books. They seem to suspect that there is some occult power in them, some mystery that they would like to grasp. My friend, who has the bearing of a prizefighter, but the heart of an amiable child, came over and picked up the book. He sat down at the table with me and looked at it. I was a little doubtful how to explain matters, for I felt that it was the kind of book he would not be likely to care for. He began spelling it out loud, rather laboriously—

Section 1. Well! Being born into this world there are, I suppose, many aims which we may strive to attain.

To my surprise he showed the greatest enthusiasm. So much so that I ordered another

[113]

pair of bran muffins, which I did not really
want, so that he might have more time for reading Kenko.

"Who was this fellow?" he asked.

"He was a Jap," I said, "lived a long time
ago. He was mighty thick with the Emperor,
and after the Emperor died he went to live by
himself in the country, and became a priest, and
wrote down his thoughts."

"I see," said my friend. "Just put down
whatever came into his head, eh?"

"That's it. All his ideas about the queer
things a fellow runs into in life, you know, little
bits of philosophy."

I was a little afraid of using that word
"philosophy," but I couldn't think of anything
else to say. It struck my friend very pleasantly.

"That's it," he said, "philosophy. Just as
you say, now, he went off by himself and put
things down the way they come to him. Philosophy. Sure. Say, that's a good kind of book.
I like that kind of thing. I have a lot of books
at home, you know. I get home about nine
o'clock, and I most always read a bit before I
go to bed."

How I yearned to know what books they were,
but it seemed rude to question him.

He dipped into Kenko again, and I wondered

whether courtesy demanded that I should order another pot of tea.

"Say, would you like to do me a favor?"

"Sure thing," I said.

"When you get through with that book, pass it over, will you? That's the kind of thing I've been wanting. Just some little thoughts, you know, something short. I've got a lot of books at home."

His big florid face gleamed with friendly earnestness.

"Sure thing," I said. "Just as soon as I've finished it you shall have it." I wanted to ask whether he would reciprocate by lending me one of his own books, which would give me some clue to his tastes; but again I felt obscurely that he would not understand my curiosity.

As I went out he called to me again from where he stood by the shining coffee boiler. "Don't forget, will you?" he said. "When you're through, just pass it over."

I promised faithfully, and tomorrow evening I shall take the book in to him. I honestly hope he'll enjoy it. I walked up the bright wintry street, and wondered what Kenko would have said to the endless flow of taxicabs, the elevators and subways, the telephones, and telegraph offices, the newsstands and especially the plate-glass windows of florists. He would have

[115]

had some urbane, cynical and delightfully dis-illusioning remarks to offer. And, as Mr. Weaver so shrewdly says, how he would enjoy "The Way of All Flesh!"

I came back to Hallbedroom street, and set down these few meditations. There is much more I would like to say, but the partitions in hall bedrooms are thin, and the lady in the next room thumps on the wall if I keep the type-writer going after ten o'clock.

TWO DAYS WE CELEBRATE

I F we were asked (we have not been asked) to name a day the world ought to celebrate and does not, we would name the 16th of May. For on that day, in the year 1763, James Boswell first met Dr. Samuel Johnson.

This great event, which enriched the world with one of the most vivid panoramas of human nature known to man, happened in Tom Davies's bookshop in Covent Garden. Mr. and Mrs. Davies were friends of the Doctor, who frequently visited their shop. Of them Boswell remarks quaintly that though they had been on the stage for many years, they "main-

[117]

tained an uniform decency of character." The shop seems to have been a charming place: one went there not merely to buy books, but also to have a cup of tea in the back parlor. It is sad to think that though we have been hanging round bookshops for a number of years, we have never yet met a bookseller who invited us into the private office for a quiet cup. Wait a moment, though, we are forgetting Dr. Rosenbach, the famous bookseller of Philadelphia. But his collations, held in amazed memory by many editioneers, rarely descend to anything so humble as tea. One recalls a confused glamor of ortolans, trussed guinea-hens, strawberries reclining in a bowl carved out of solid ice, and what used to be known as vintages. It is a pity that Dr. Johnson died too soon to take lunch with Dr. Rosenbach.

"At last, on Monday, the 16th of May," says Boswell, "when I was sitting in Mr. Davies's back parlor, after having drunk tea with him and Mrs. Davies, Johnson unexpectedly came into the shop; and Mr. Davies, having perceived him through the glass door, announced his awful approach to me. Mr. Davies mentioned my name, and respectfully introduced me to him. I was much agitated." The volatile Boswell may be forgiven his agitation. We also would have trembled not a little. Boswell was only twenty-two, and probably felt that his whole life and career hung upon the great man's mood. But embarrassment is a comely emotion for a young man in the face of greatness; and the Doctor was speedily put in a good humor by an opportunity to utter his favorite pleasantry at the expense of the Scotch. "I do, indeed, come from Scotland," cried Boswell, after Davies had let the cat out of the bag; "but I cannot help it." "That, sir," said Doctor Johnson, "is what a great many of your countrymen cannot help."

The great book that dated from that meeting in Davies's back parlor has become one of the most intimately cherished possessions of the race. One finds its admirers and students scattered over the globe. No man who loves human nature in all its quirks and pangs, seasoned with bluff honesty and the genuineness of a cliff or a tree, can afford to step into a hearse until he has made it his own. And it is a noteworthy illustration of the biblical saying that whosoever will rule, let him be a servant. Boswell made himself the servant of Johnson, and became one of the masters of English literature.

It used to annoy us to hear Karl Rosner referred to as "the Kaiser's Boswell." For to *boswellize* (which is a verb that has gone into

our dictionaries) means not merely to transcribe
faithfully the acts and moods and import of a
man's life; it implies also that the man so delineated be a good man and a great. Horace
Traubel was perhaps a Boswell; but Rosner,
never.

It is pleasant to know that Boswell was not
merely a kind of animated note-book. He was
a droll, vain, erring, bibulous, warm-hearted
creature, a good deal of a Pepys, in fact, with
all the Pepysian vices and virtues. Mr. A. Ed-
ward Newton's "Amenities of Book Collecting"
makes Boswell very human to us. How jolly it
is to learn that Jamie (like many lesser fry
since) wrote press notices about himself. Here
is one of his own blurbs, which we quote from
Mr. Newton's book:

Boswell, the author, is a most excellent man: he is
of an ancient family in the west of Scotland, upon
which he values himself not a little. At his nativity
there appeared omens of his future greatness. His
parts are bright, and his education has been good.
He has traveled in post chaises miles without number. He is fond of seeing much of the world. He
eats of every good dish, especially apple pie. He
drinks Old Hock. He has a very fine temper. He
is somewhat of a humorist and a little tinctured with
pride. He has a good manly countenance, and he
owns himself to be amorous. He has infinite viva-
city, yet is observed at times to have a melancholy

cast. He is rather fat than lean, rather short than
tall, rather young than old. His shoes are neatly
made, and he never wears spectacles.

This brings the excellent Boswell very close
to us indeed: he might almost be a member of
the Authors' League. "Especially apple pie,
bless his heart!"

When we said that Boswell was a kind of
Pepys, we fell by chance into a happy compari-
son. Not only by his volatile errors was he of
the tribe of Samuel, but in his outstanding
character by which he becomes of importance to
posterity—that of one of the great diarists.
Now there is no human failing upon which we
look with more affectionate lenience than that
of keeping a diary. All of us, in our pilgrim-
age through the difficult thickets of this world,
have moods and moments when we have to fall
back on ourselves for the only complete understanding and absolution we will ever find.
In such times, how pleasant it is to record our
emotions and misgivings in the sure and secret
pages of some privy notebook; and how enter-
taining to read them again in later years! Dr.
Johnson himself advised Bozzy to keep a journal, though he little suspected to what use it
would be put. The cynical will say that he did
so in order that Bozzy would have less time to

[121]

pester him, but we believe his advice was sincere. It must have been, for the Doctor kept one himself, of which more in a moment.

"He recommended to me," Boswell says, "to keep a journal of my life, full and unreserved. He said it would be a very good exercise and would yield me great satisfaction when the particulars were faded from my remembrance. He counselled me to keep it private, and said I might surely have a friend who would burn it in case of my death."

Happily it was not burned. The Great Doctor never seemed so near to me as the other day when I saw a little notebook, bound in soft brown leather and interleaved with blotting paper, in which Bozzy's busy pen had jotted down memoranda of his talks with his friend, while they were still echoing in his mind. From this notebook (which must have been one of many) the paragraphs were transferred practically unaltered into the Life. This superb treasure, now owned by Mr. Adam of Buffalo, almost makes one hear the Doctor's voice; and one imagines Boswell sitting up at night with his candle, methodically recording the remarks of the day. The first entry was dated September 22, 1777, so Bozzy must have carried it in his pocket when Dr. Johnson and he were visiting Dr. Taylor in Ashbourne. It was during this

junket that Dr. Johnson tried to pole the large
dead cat over Dr. Taylor's dam, an incident
that Boswell recorded as part of his "Flemish
picture of my friend." It was then also that
Mrs. Killingley, mistress of Ashbourne's lead-
ing inn, The Green Man, begged Boswell "to
name the house to his extensive acquaintance."
Certainly Bozzy's acquaintance was to be far
more extensive than good Mrs. Killingley ever
dreamed. It was he who "named the house"
to me, and for this reason The Green Man
profited in fourpence worth of cider, 134 years
later.

There is another day we have vowed to com-
memorate, by drinking great flaggonage of tea,
and that is the 18th of September, Dr. Johnson's birthday. The Great Cham needs no
champion; his speech and person have become
part of our common heritage. Yet the extraordinary scenario in which Boswell filmed him for
us has attained that curious estate of great literature the characteristic of which is that every
man imagines he has read it, though he may
never have opened its pages. It is like the his-
toric landmark of one's home town, which for-
eigners from overseas come to study, but which
the denizen has hardly entered. It is like Niagara Falls: we have a very fair mental picture of
the spectacle and little zeal to visit the

[123]

uproar itself. And so, though we all use Doctor Johnson's sharply stamped coinages, we generally are too lax about visiting the mint.

But we will never cease to pray that every honest man should study Boswell. There are many who have topped the rise of human felicity in that book: when reading it they feel the tide of intellect brim the mind with a unique fullness of satisfaction. It is not a mere commentary on life: it *is* life—it fills and floods every channel of the brain. It is a book that men make a hobby of, as golf or billiards. To know it is a liberal education. I could have understood Germany yearning to invade England in order to annex Boswell's Johnson. There would have been some sense in that.

What is the average man's conception of Doctor Johnson? We think of a huge ungainly creature, slovenly of dress, addicted to tea, the author of a dictionary and the center of a tavern coterie. We think of him prefacing bluff and vehement remarks with "Sir," and having a knack for demolishing opponents in boisterous argument. All of which is passing true, just as is our picture of the Niagara we have never seen; but how it misses the inner tenderness and tormented virtue of the man!

So it is refreshing sometimes to turn away from Boswell to those passages where the good

[124]

Two Days We Celebrate

old Doctor has revealed himself with his own hand. The letter to Chesterfield is too well known for comment. But no less noble, and not nearly so well known, is the preface to the Dictionary. How moving it is in its sturdy courage, its strong grasp of the tools of expression. In every line one feels the weight and push of a mind that had behind it the full reservoir of language, particularly the Latin. There is the same sense of urgent pressure that one feels in watching a strong stream backed up behind a dam:

I look with pleasure on my book, however defective, and deliver it to the world with the spirit of a man that has endeavored well. That it will immediately become popular I have not promised to myself: a few wild blunders, and risible absurdities, from which no work of such multiplicity was ever free, may for a time furnish folly with laughter, and harden ignorance in contempt, but useful diligence will at last prevail, and there never can be wanting some who distinguish desert; who will consider that no dictionary of a living tongue ever can be perfect, since while it is hastening to publication, some words are budding, and some falling away; that a whole life cannot be spent upon syntax and etymology, and that even a whole life would not be sufficient; that he, whose design includes whatever language can express, must often speak of what he does not understand; that a writer will sometimes be hurried by eagerness to the end, and sometimes faint

[125]

with weariness under a task, which Scaliger compares to the labors of the anvil and the mine; that what is obvious is not always known, and what is known is not always present; that sudden fits of inadvertency will surprise vigilance, slight avocations will seduce attention, and casual eclipses of the mind will darken learning; and that the writer shall often in vain trace his memory at the moment of need, for that which yesterday he knew with intuitive readiness, and which will come uncalled into his thoughts to-morrow.

I know no better way of celebrating Doctor Johnson's birthday than by quoting a few passages from his "Prayers and Meditations," jotted down during his life in small note-books and given shortly before his death to a friend. No one understands the dear old doctor unless he remembers that his spirit was greatly perplexed and harassed by sad and disordered broodings. The bodily twitchings and odd gestures which attracted so much attention as he rolled about the streets were symptoms of painful twitchings and gestures within. A great part of his intense delight in convivial gatherings, in conversation and the dinner table, was due to his eagerness to be taken out of himself. One fears that his solitary hours were very often tragic.

There were certain dates which Doctor Johnson almost always commemorated in his private

Street, is the oddest plumber's shop in the world. Mr. George F. Hammond, a Civil War veteran, who knew Whitman and also Lincoln, came to Camden in '69. In 1888 he determined to build a shop that would be different from anything on earth, and well he succeeded. Perhaps it is symbolic of the shy and harassed soul of the plumber, fleeing from the unreasonable demands of his customers, for it is a kind of Gothic fortress. Leaded windows, gargoyles, masculine medusa heads, a sallyport, loopholes and a little spire. I stopped in to talk to Mr. Hammond, and he greeted me graciously. He says that people have come all the way from California to see his shop, and I can believe it. It is the work of a delightful and original spirit who does not care to live in a demure hutch like all the rest of us, and has really had some fun out of his whimsical little castle. He says he would rather live in Camden than in Philadelphia, and I daresay he's right.

III

Something in his aspect as he leaned over the railing near me drew me on to speak to him. I don't know just how to describe it except by saying that he had an understanding look. He gave me the impression of a man who had spent his life in thinking and would understand me,

ON DOORS

THE opening and closing of doors are the most significant actions of man's life. What a mystery lies in doors!

No man knows what awaits him when he opens a door. Even the most familiar room, where the clock ticks and the hearth glows red at dusk, may harbor surprises. The plumber may actually have called (while you were out) and fixed that leaking faucet. The cook may have had a fit of the vapors and demanded her passports. The wise man opens his front door with humility and a spirit of acceptance.

Which one of us has not sat in some ante-room and watched the inscrutable panels of a door that was full of meaning? Perhaps you were waiting to apply for a job; perhaps you had some "deal" you were ambitious to put over. You watched the confidential stenographer flit in and out, carelessly turning that mystic portal which, to you, revolved on hinges of fate. And then the young woman said, "Mr. Cranberry will see you now." As you grasped

On Doors

the knob the thought flashed, "When I open this door again, what will have happened?"

There are many kinds of doors. Revolving doors for hotels, shops and public buildings. These are typical of the brisk, bustling ways of modern life. Can you imagine John Milton or William Penn skipping through a revolving door? Then there are the curious little slatted doors that still swing outside denatured barrooms and extend only from shoulder to knee. There are trapdoors, sliding doors, double doors, stage doors, prison doors, glass doors. But the symbol and mystery of a door resides in its quality of concealment. A glass door is not a door at all, but a window. The meaning of a door is to hide what lies inside; to keep the heart in suspense.

Also, there are many ways of opening doors. There is the cheery push of elbow with which the waiter shoves open the kitchen door when he bears in your tray of supper. There is the suspicious and tentative withdrawal of a door before the unhappy book agent or peddler. There is the genteel and carefully modulated recession with which footmen swing wide the oaken barriers of the great. There is the sympathetic and awful silence of the dentist's maid who opens the door into the operating

think then, one hopes, of our unfulfilled decencies rather than of our pluperfected misdemeanors. Then they will go out and close the door.